AF823490

SIDREA Series in Accounting and Business Administration

Series Editors

Stefano Marasca, Università Politecnica delle Marche, Ancona, Italy

Anna Maria Fellegara, Università Cattolica del Sacro Cuore, Piacenza, Italy

Riccardo Mussari, Università di Siena, Siena, Italy

Editorial Board

Stefano Adamo, University of Lecce, Leece, Italy

Luca Bartocci, University of Perugia, Perugia, Italy

Adele Caldarelli, University of Naples Federico II, Naples, Italy

Bettina Campedelli, University of Verona, Verona, Italy

Nicola Castellano, University of Pisa, Pisa, Italy

Denita Cepiku, University of Rome Tor Vergata, Rome, Italy

Lino Cinquini, Sant'Anna School of Advanced Studies, Pisa, Italy

Maria Serena Chiucchi, Marche Polytechnic University, Ancona, Italy

Vittorio Dell'Atti, University of Bari Aldo Moro, Bari, Italy

Francesco De Luca, University of Chieti-Pescara, Pescara, Italy

Anna Maria Fellegara, Catholic University of the Sacred Heart, Piacenza, Italy

Raffaele Fiorentino, University of Naples Parthenope, Naples, Italy

Francesco Giunta, University of Florence, Florence, Italy

Alberto Incollingo, University of Campania "Luigi Vanvitelli", Caserta, Italy

Giovanni Liberatore, University of Florence, Florence, Italy

Andrea Lionzo, Catholic University of the Sacred Heart, Milano, Italy

Rosa Lombardi, University of Rome, Sapienza, Roma, Italy

Davide Maggi, Amedeo Avogadro University of Eastern Piedmont, Novara, Italy

Daniela Mancini, University of Teramo, Teramo, Italy

Francesca Manes Rossi, University of Naples Federico II, Naples, Italy

Luciano Marchi, University of Pisa, Pisa, Italy

Riccardo Mussari, University of Siena, Siena, Italy

Marco Maria Mattei, University of Bologna, Forlì, Italy

Antonella Paolini, University of Macerata, Macerata, Italy

Mauro Paoloni, University of Rome Tor Vergata, Rome, Italy

Paola Paoloni, University of Rome Tor Vergata, Rome, Italy, Sapienza University of Rome, Rome, Italy

Marcantonio Ruisi, University of Palermo, Palermo, Italy

Claudio Teodori, University of Brescia, Brescia, Italy

Simone Terzani, University of Perugia, Perugia, Italy

Stefania Veltri, University of Calabria, Rende, Italy

This is the official book series of SIDREA - the Italian Society of Accounting and Business Administration. This book series is provided with a wide Scientific Committee composed of Academics by SIDREA. It publishes contributions (monographs, edited volumes and proceedings) as a result of the double blind review process by the SIDREA's thematic research groups, operating at the national and international levels. Particularly, the series aims to disseminate specialized findings on several topics – classical and cutting-edge alike – that are currently being discussed by the accounting and business administration communities. The series authors are respected researchers and professors in the fields of business valuation; governance and internal control; financial accounting; public accounting; management control; gender; turnaround predictive models; non-financial disclosure; intellectual capital, smart technologies, and digitalization; and university governance and performance measurement.This book series is indexed in Scopus.

Sara Longo

Disclosure in Banking

The Role of Financial Reporting in Bank Behaviors and Investor Decision-Making

Springer

Sara Longo
Free University of Bozen-Bolzano
Bolzano, Italy

ISSN 2662-9879 ISSN 2662-9887 (electronic)
SIDREA Series in Accounting and Business Administration
ISBN 978-3-031-84195-8 ISBN 978-3-031-84196-5 (eBook)
https://doi.org/10.1007/978-3-031-84196-5

© The Editor(s) (if applicable) and The Author(s), under exclusive license to Springer Nature Switzerland AG 2025
This work is subject to copyright. All rights are solely and exclusively licensed by the Publisher, whether the whole or part of the material is concerned, specifically the rights of translation, reprinting, reuse of illustrations, recitation, broadcasting, reproduction on microfilms or in any other physical way, and transmission or information storage and retrieval, electronic adaptation, computer software, or by similar or dissimilar methodology now known or hereafter developed.
The use of general descriptive names, registered names, trademarks, service marks, etc. in this publication does not imply, even in the absence of a specific statement, that such names are exempt from the relevant protective laws and regulations and therefore free for general use.
The publisher, the authors and the editors are safe to assume that the advice and information in this book are believed to be true and accurate at the date of publication. Neither the publisher nor the authors or the editors give a warranty, expressed or implied, with respect to the material contained herein or for any errors or omissions that may have been made. The publisher remains neutral with regard to jurisdictional claims in published maps and institutional affiliations.

This Springer imprint is published by the registered company Springer Nature Switzerland AG
The registered company address is: Gewerbestrasse 11, 6330 Cham, Switzerland

If disposing of this product, please recycle the paper.

To Diego and Luca

Preface

The recent bank failures of Silicon Valley Bank and Credit Suisse in March 2023 have highlighted the importance and the questionable fragility of disclosure by linking accounting practices with financial stability. At that time, the convictions of having learned the lesson from the biggest financial crisis of 2007-08 disappeared very quickly, and a new debate started again about how to achieve transparency through mandated disclosure mechanisms. The banking industry has been the most regulated sector compared to other industries, and this depends on the opacity featured, particularly in the banking world. Prior literature proposes a huge number of theoretical, empirical, and experimental studies about disclosure. Mostly, they are split on examining disclosure based on a corporate voluntary initiative, alternatively to a regulatory mandate. Banks are involved in disclosing information any time the regulator requires them to do it, and at the same time, any time managers need to inform capital markets' players about important decisions or achievements. Notwithstanding the possibility of identifying better effects in one case instead of the other, voluntary and mandatory disclosures could lead to detrimental effects. Banks also like playing opportunistically by shifting from mandatory to voluntary disclosure, especially when they need to cover bad news. Further studies are focused on examining mandated disclosure leading to spillover effects when a group of firms obliged to disclose specific information push other firms (not obliged) to do so voluntarily, with the final results of obtaining a more transparent informational environment.

Disclosure plays a fundamental economic role in mitigating agency conflicts in light of information asymmetries between managers and capital markets participants. However, different from common expectations, bankers are much more aligned with shareholders' interests and much less with the regulators and supervisors. The financial crisis of 2007-08 taught us that a banking crash can provoke contagion effects first on the entire banking sector and then on the real sector, especially when banks are not transparent. At that time, higher levels of disclosure would have mitigated the severity of the crisis consequences. Disclosure cannot automatically lead to more transparency. Nevertheless, in the aftermath of the crisis, regulators decided to revise and issue new rules to avoid future failure risks. Most of these rules were dedicated to improving risk disclosure from accounting and banking perspectives. Nowadays banks should be compliant and provide consistent information useful to overcome important tests linked to financial stability and asset quality based on more accurate and timely financial accounting information than in the past (i.e., stress tests and transparency exercises). Regulators and supervisors are continuously involved in ascertaining the health of banks, especially the significant ones. The need to have transparent banks affects not only their financial stability but also their levels of competition. Financial institutions should also improve their transparency to contribute effectively to the decarbonization process toward reducing corporate GHG emissions. This call has come up in light of the urgency of climate change risk affecting human lives and the economy. The banking sector plays a significant role in fostering sustainable development as a core area of economic operation and a cutting-edge, clean services sector.

On the wave of these considerations, this monograph reviews the academic literature examining the role of disclosure in the banking industry, balancing transparency with stability, competition, and lending activity as the main source of bank profits. Then, it proposes dedicated sections to systematically know how these aspects have been studied theoretically and empirically, focusing on the measurement approaches. In the last part of this monograph, I conduct an empirical investigation leveraging the contribution of the recent climate stress tests on a group of banks doing green lending. I examine whether more transparent banks lend more, prioritizing borrowers' ESG disclosure. The main findings suggest that banks scrutinized by the European Banking Authority (EBA) to verify the assessment of climate risk exposure are more prone to issue sustainability-linked and green loans.

This book can interest both experienced and early-stage scholars focusing on banking disclosure. Overall, it offers valuable insights into how disclosure has contributed to well-functioning capital markets, mitigating bank failure risks. In the past, banks have received low attention regarding their climate change response due to their lower direct emissions of greenhouse gases compared to other industries. This book enhances how banks promote a green economy by employing borrowers' ESG disclosure in their lending activity and disclosing their climate change risk exposure to their supervisors, like the ECB.

Bolzano, Italy Sara Longo

Acknowledgments

Thanks to the Società Italiana dei Docenti di Ragioneria e di Economia Aziendale (SIDREA) and the anonymous reviewers for their valuable comments. I am grateful to Prof. Massimiliano Bonacchi (Free University of Bolzano) for his support, advice, and patience in following me during my writing and these last six years. I also want to thank my Ph.D. supervisors, Prof. Antonio Parbonetti (University of Padova) and Prof. Amedeo Pugliese (University of Padova), for providing helpful comments and being important guides from the beginning of my academic career. I found inspiration to write this book during the Accounting Summer Camps of the joint collaboration of the Free University of Bolzano and the University of Padova (V^ edition at the University Pompeu Fabra—Spain, and VI^ edition at the University of Padova—Italy) after some insightful talks with Prof. Stefano Cascino (London School of Economics) and Prof. Joachim Gassen (Humboldt Frei Universität). I want to thank them for inspiring me and assessing the aim of this book. Last but not least, my thanks go to Prof. Claudia Curi (Free University of Bolzano) for mentoring me with her banking and corporate finance expertise. For supporting me during this hard work thanks go to Olga Bogachek and Giulia Gastaldello.

All errors and omissions are the sole responsibility of the author.

Contents

Chapter 1
Introduction

1.1 Motivation and Objectives of This Book

In this book, I provide a comprehensive overview of the implications of disclosure (particularly disclosure regulation) in the banking industry. As academics, policymakers, and professionals in the banking industry, understanding this topic is crucial. I first highlight why disclosure matters in banking, bridging transparency, financial stability, and competition. Disclosure regulation plays a key part in well-functioning capital markets. Regulators often mandate new disclosure requirements to either improve the flow of information to a society or encourage a desired behavior. In that sense, the banking industry is no exception. In the aftermath of the financial crisis of 2007–2008, policymakers promoted disclosure regulation to enhance the transparency of the financial system. This financial crisis cemented a widespread belief that banking institutions were not sufficiently transparent when less opacity in banks' financial reporting would have probably mitigated the consequences of the biggest financial crisis in human history (Barth & Landsman, 2010). It has mostly witnessed the complexity of the impacts of regulated disclosure on increasing transparency-stability for banks. Disclosure regulation can reduce uncertainty and increase transparency, such as the availability of bank-specific, value-relevant information to external stakeholders (Bushman, 2014; Bushman & Williams, 2012). Understanding the information environment and the economic context becomes crucial every time a researcher intends to investigate whether and to what extent investors could perceive a further mandated disclosure regulation and how it could shape their financial-economic decisions. Indeed, the power of disclosure regulation lies in enabling banks to better manage risk exposure in order to reduce opacity, consequently leading to a lower cost of capital and higher contracting efficiency (Armstrong et al., 2010; Healy & Palepu, 2001). However, this is not always the case; in fact, there are several exceptions to consider when transparency represents an issue:

© The Author(s), under exclusive license to Springer Nature Switzerland AG 2025

S. Longo, *Disclosure in Banking*, SIDREA Series in Accounting and Business Administration, https://doi.org/10.1007/978-3-031-84196-5_1

- Banks experience temporary and recoverable weaknesses (Nier, 2005).
- As the level of noise in mandatory disclosure increases, investors may return to valuing voluntary disclosure (Einhorn, 2005).
- Timely and accurate bank disclosure indicates widespread problems, leading to bank runs (Bryant, 1980; Diamond & Dybvig, 1983).

Grounded in regulatory disclosure, transparency is essential to promoting and guaranteeing financial stability (transparency-stability view). Increased transparency generally enhances market discipline, whereas bank transparency increases the sensitivity of banks' funding terms to the risk they take (Bushman, 2014; Bushman & Williams, 2012). Risks and monitoring efforts are accurately observable when transparency increases (Nier, 2005; Boot & Schmeits, 2000; Cordella & Yeyati, 1998). However, managerial discretion can facilitate the incorporation of private information that supports the bank's lending activity. Still, this discretion increases the potential for opportunism by managers (agency problems), increasing opacity and leading to investor uncertainty about banks' intrinsic value, which in turn weakens market discipline over risk-taking behavior.

The banking industry has recently started to face new shocks, which are different from their previous financial experiences. Indeed, today's banking industry should be aware of the consequences of the increased frequency of natural disasters as an outcome of climate change (Gourdel et al., 2022), which was particularly highlighted during the 2020 pandemic crisis (Berger & Demirgüç-Kunt, 2021). The pandemic crisis has emphasized the need to rebuild economies and societies more sustainably and resiliently by investing in green technologies and renewable energies aimed at decarbonization. In this book, I propose a comprehensive overview of how banks use environmental disclosure in their lending activities and how they provide environmental disclosure to markets. Following recent research studies, I identify how banks become "green" and how environmental disclosure has been identified and measured. Then based on these considerations, I conduct an empirical investigation to examine whether environmental disclosure through the European Banking Authority's (EBA's) climate stress tests affects the growth of banks' "green" lending (Monasterolo et al., 2020). Particularly, I leverage the new challenging rules for banks that have heightened their focus on assessing and addressing climate-related risks. Indeed, empirical data indicates that banks are progressively attuned to environmental concerns in a broader sense (Degryse et al., 2021). Insights into the financial ramifications of climate change underscore the multifaceted nature of these consequences, encompassing physical risks, transition risks arising from climate-induced innovations, and regulatory risks. I choose climate stress tests because banks, particularly central banks (i.e., the European Banking Authority), know that climate change is not just an environmental concern. It also presents substantial financial risks associated with disasters that can damage infrastructure, properties, and businesses, causing significant economic losses. Climate change risk is on the agenda of each bank since it can affect financial stability, leading to a contagion effect. Banks have always been considered black boxes, but in light of natural disaster risks, it seems that this time, they have no other way of avoiding transparency through disclosure regulation.

This monograph contributes to prior literature in three ways:

1) First, it reviews the academic literature, examining the importance of disclosure in banking markets. Here, I highlight how disclosure increases transparency, financial stability, and competition in the banking industry. This sector is characterized by complexity, and the coordination of regulation, supervision, and enforcement creates various paces, depending on the bank's characteristics.
2) Second, this monograph presents insights into the fragile link between accounting practices and disclosure in assessing financial stability. Bankers have superior information relative to investors and other stakeholders regarding default risks inherent in their loan portfolios. Thus, they discretionally signal the bank's stability and profitability to investors, playing around with loans' portfolio quality.
3) Disclosure is a powerful tool that can act as a deterrent against banks' failures and mitigate the severity of the consequences of crises. New forms of disclosure are dedicated to the banking industry. This book highlights how the disclosure from recent climate stress tests conducted by the European Central Bank on a group of listed banks can serve as a significant step toward decarbonization, directly engaging lenders with their borrowers. Although full transparency can trigger bank runs, sustainability-focused transparency helps banks reduce their credit losses and maintain their financial stability. By embracing these changes, we can look forward to a more resilient and sustainable banking industry.

The book is based on five chapters (including this chapter, which is dedicated to the introduction). In the following table (Table 1.1), I propose a map of how I proceed with my examination:

Table 1.1 A map to read this book

Topic	Chapter
In this chapter, I first describe the importance of disclosure regulation in the banking industry. After understanding the role of regulation as complementary to market discipline, I provide an insightful literature review on regulated disclosure for transparency, financial stability, and competition.	Chapter 2
This chapter focuses on the fragile link between accounting practices and disclosure in maintaining financial stability. I leverage the complexity to coordinate rules based on two different approaches: accounting and prudential.	Chapter 3
In this chapter, I present the required disclosures for the banking industry in response to increasing adverse events, like natural disasters, that could affect banks' financial stability. I provide an overview of the growing environmental disclosures, ESG rating approaches, green lending, and climate stress test disclosure at the bank level, focusing on green disclosure.	Chapter 4
In this chapter, I conduct an empirical investigation using a sample of listed eurozone banks that offer green lending. I empirically test whether the first examination of the European Banking Authority's (EBA, 2020) climate stress test affects the growth of green lending. I present the empirical results and my contribution according to prior literature.	Chapter 5
In this chapter, I offer concluding remarks on this monograph, suggesting potential avenues for future research.	Chapter 6

1.2 Banking Disclosure

Disclosure regulation for banks is fundamental to enabling ordinary, stable operations in financial systems. Regulated disclosure for the banking industry has been strongly debated and contemporarily advocated since banks:

1) Play a fundamental economic role in supporting the real sector (Bossone, 2001)
2) Like leveraging and tend to increase their risk-taking behavior (Laeven & Levine, 2009)
3) Can contaminate the entire financial system when they fail, which can lead to further severe consequences for the real economy, implying heavy welfare social costs (Granja, 2013).

Mandatory disclosure is preferred for banks, as voluntary disclosure may not always be in the best interest of capital markets participants, since bank managers might withhold crucial bad information generating agency problems (i.e., the issue of the information asymmetry). Bankers view disclosures as costly by nature and weigh these costs against the potential benefits of lower funding costs when determining the quality, level and frequency of disclosures. Moreover, they use considerable discretion in deciding what information to disclose, which also means that voluntary disclosures may not necessarily generate optimal outcomes (Landsman, 2007). In the aftermath of the financial crisis of 2007–2008, regulators have advocated for more stringent disclosure requirements for financial institutions. Thus, bank disclosure concerning financial and risk information is an important mechanism for improving market efficiency through various channels:

1) It serves as an outside mechanism for monitoring the behavior of senior management (Eng & Mak, 2003).
2) It lowers investors' uncertainty about a firm's expected future cash flows and enables public firms to access external finance at a reasonable cost of capital (Botosan, 1997; Botosan & Plumlee, 2002).
3) It supports the firm's legitimacy and reputation, thus maintaining the trust of various stakeholders (Lindblom, 1994).

Bischof (2009) argues that financial risk disclosure is most relevant to banks, considering the nature of their activities, where financial instruments constitute more than 90% of their total assets and liabilities. However, scholars claim that financial risk disclosures by banks are largely unclear and incomprehensible. Indeed, readability represents a significant issue, and researchers are focusing on understanding risk disclosures better by employing several techniques:

- Quantitative methods such as balance sheet data and financial indicators (Kapan & Minoiu, 2018; Zeghal & Lahmar, 2016; Frankel et al., 2016)
- Content analysis (Maffei et al., 2014; Ibrahim & Hussainey, 2019; Lamanda & Tamasne Voneki, 2020; Polizzi, 2022; Lajili et al., 2022; Scannella & Polizzi, 2021)

- Quantitative and qualitative methods by constructing a graphical accuracy index (Jones et al., 2018)
- Textual analysis (Del Gaudio et al., 2020)

However, what we learned from the biggest financial crisis (2007–2008) was insufficient to prevent further bank crises. Indeed, the recent bank failures (i.e., Silicon Valley Bank and Credit Suisse in March 2023) have highlighted the importance of properly disclosed risks to allow investors to evaluate a bank's risk profile (Bischof et al., 2021). Due to the specificities of banks' activities, banks are more opaque than nonfinancial firms (Flannery et al., 2013; Morgan, 2002). It is noteworthy that, in the absence of information, moral hazard problems might negatively affect the value of banks since managers might act against the interests of investors, which can impact the global economy.

The success of any new disclosure requirements depends on the written rules and how regulators and the firms they regulate implement and adhere to these rules. In particular, public enforcement is often seen as an important determinant of the effectiveness of financial reporting regulation (e.g., Holthausen, 2009; Christensen et al., 2017). One important aspect of public enforcement is the choice and structure of supervisory institutions. A specialized industry regulator often exists besides the securities market regulator responsible for designing and monitoring the disclosure regime. Having multiple regulators should not affect the effectiveness of their supervisory activities as they all have in mind the overall well-being of financial markets and their constituents. Different regulators may follow their own agendas and have different views on the role of transparency in functioning capital markets (e.g., Flannery, 2020). On the other hand, multiple supervisory agencies are simultaneously tasked with overlapping responsibilities. A good example is that IFRS 7 requires disclosures about the nature and extent of risks arising from financial instruments, and it applies to all firms subject to IFRS reporting. Its enforcement generally lies with the agency supervising national securities markets and is sometimes delegated to a third party, like the local stock exchange. With the third pillar of the Basel II Accord (Pillar 3), the Basel Committee on Banking Supervision issued risk disclosure requirements, which, in many aspects, are equivalent to IFRS 7 but fall under the auspices of the national banking supervisor (Mies, 2024; Bischof et al., 2022). We recognize that the regulatory framework for banks may produce unintended effects and may not always be effective. However, if a bank provides more disclosures to a greater number of entities, it becomes more transparent, which in turn promotes greater financial stability. Public enforcement implies that a supervisory agency imposes costly sanctions on firms that deviate from intended reporting practices, thereby providing economic incentives for firms to apply specific rules in their desired way (Shleifer, 2005). Different agencies (e.g., the Federal Deposit Insurance Corporation (FDIC), the Federal Reserve System, and the Office of the Comptroller of the Currency (OCC)) are charged with bank supervision to maintain a safe and sound banking system through on-site examinations. When these on-site examinations suggest unsafe, unsound, or illegal practices that violate laws, enforcement actions are used to restore safety and soundness by altering bank practices, stabilizing institutions, and averting losses to deposit insurers (Danisewicz et al., 2018).

Recent years have witnessed the growing adoption of frameworks such as TCFD (Task Force on Climate-Related Financial Disclosures) recommendations by banks (June 2017), which focus on enhancing transparency and facilitating informed decision-making. This involves transparently reporting climate-related risks and opportunities and incorporating climate considerations into governance and risk management frameworks. Governments worldwide are implementing regulations to curtail greenhouse gas emissions and encourage sustainable practices. These regulatory measures can impact various aspects of banking operations:

- Risk management strategies
- Capital requirements
- Disclosure obligations

Moreover, banks indirectly encounter regulatory risks linked to climate change through their loan portfolios, impacting credit allocation choices. Thus, banks exposed to "stranded assets," such as assets grounded on fossil fuel reserves or coal-fired power plants that are economically unsustainable, may face significant financial risks, including collateral devaluation and potential loan defaults. Banks may also be susceptible to reputational harm, legal actions, or disinvestment campaigns initiated by stakeholders advocating for more robust climate-related actions. The aim is to diversify loan portfolios by augmenting investments in low-carbon sectors, including renewable energy, energy efficiency, and sustainable infrastructure. The expected outcome is to help shift banks' focus, reducing their vulnerability to high-carbon sectors and aligning their lending practices with low-carbon objectives (Dursun-de Neef et al., 2023; Giannetti et al., 2023; Kim et al., 2023; Wang, 2023). The goal is to see the gradual production of environmental and, more broadly, non-financial disclosures from banks, which investors should be able to incorporate into their decision-making process regarding capital allocation choices.

1.3 The Need to Do Research on Disclosure

Banks' disclosure practices are influenced by strategic, discretionary decisions, regulatory incentives, and market pressures, with variations depending on ownership structure. For instance, banks owned by major shareholders like BlackRock, Vanguard, and State Street may disclose differently from state-owned banks. Researchers have sought to understand why banks voluntarily disclose information beyond regulatory requirements. Voluntary disclosure is typically seen as a means for organizations to justify their activities, conform to social norms, and manage stakeholder expectations (Grossman & Hart, 1980; Milgrom, 1981; Verrecchia, 1983, 2001). A survey by Graham, Harvey, and Rajgopal (2005) found that managers tend to provide voluntary disclosure to reduce the information risk perceived by investors. Policymakers often argue that improving the quality and quantity of disclosures through regulation reduces information asymmetry. However, empirical evidence shows that certain disclosure events can actually increase information asymmetry (Krinsky & Lee, 1996; Coller & Yohn, 1997).

The challenge of distinguishing between mandatory and voluntary disclosure is a key issue in both analytical and empirical studies of disclosure. For example, Bischof and Daske (2013) found that a mandatory one-time disclosure led to increased voluntary disclosures about sovereign risk in subsequent periods and improved the liquidity of bank shares. This finding is consistent with studies examining the determinants of voluntary disclosure and the impact of disclosure regulation (Leuz & Wysocki, 2008; Beyer et al., 2010; Bushman & Landsman, 2010; Berger, 2011). However, researchers face difficulties in assessing the effects of mandated disclosures due to endogeneity concerns, as disclosure changes are rarely random, making it challenging to draw definitive conclusions about causality (Balakrishnan et al., 2014).

1.4 Mapping Theories and Empirical Studies on Disclosure

Banks' theories can be divided into different areas, from the role of information asymmetry to delegated monitoring associated with agency problems, on one side, and equity capital, on the other. Freixas and Rochet (2008) argue that the absence of a microeconomic theory of banking before 1980 can be attributed to the unique economic role of banks, which cannot be explained within the complete market assumption of the Arrow-Debreu general equilibrium model. They demonstrate that in a competitive equilibrium, where firms and households have unrestricted access to perfect financial markets, banks would make zero profit, and the size and composition of their balance sheets would not impact other economic agents. This underscores the importance of asymmetric information between borrowers and depositors in understanding banks' delegated monitoring and deposit-taking roles. Information asymmetry is a key factor in the context of agency problems between managers and shareholders, and it can lead to increased costs of issuing outside equity and raising regulatory capital. Financial reporting potentially provides a mechanism for addressing agency problems that arise from asymmetric information. The role of accounting information is to assess the bank's monitoring of borrowers by addressing agency problems between managers and shareholders, and to serve as a foundation for capital regulation. Dang et al. (2017) argue that policies designed to enhance bank transparency negatively affect banks' ability to produce money. These recent theories, which have not been considered in the empirical accounting literature, provide potentially interesting alternative hypotheses about desirable accounting properties in the banking industry. Starting from the need to provide proper monitoring and risk-taking incentives, it is evident that accounting research should consider using accounting discretion to manage reported regulatory capital. Thus, focusing on the debate on whether the cost of outside equity depends on information asymmetry, it is necessary to recognize the relevance of information asymmetry to the cost of equity capital.

Information asymmetry reduction is at the core of disclosure theory. Based on the game theory, any entity will disclose information that is favorable and withhold that which is unfavorable (Dye, 2001). Theories tend to explain voluntary disclosure better than mandatory disclosure because they operate at the level of the individual firm (or managers) (Schipper, 2007). Both Dye (1985) and Verrecchia (1990) demonstrate that when the manager is more likely to be informed or has higher quality information, the market is more likely to interpret nondisclosure as bad news. After all, managers tend to withhold bad news when their disclosure preferences are not aligned with those of shareholders, leveraging an agency problem. Kothari et al. (2009) argue that career concerns and personal wealth at stake encourage managers to withhold bad news, while Kasznik and Lev (1995) and Skinner (1994, 1997) show that litigation risk and reputational concerns motivate managers to release bad news quickly. The full disclosure theory suggests that the threshold level of disclosure collapses to the least favorable possible information (Grossman, 1981; Milgrom, 1981; Verrecchia, 1983), implying that managers are always better off disclosing bad news as long as the bad news is better than the least favorable possible information. Understanding the managerial tendency to disclose or withhold bad news is important because a delay in bad news disclosure increases information asymmetry and worsens the firm's information environment. Prior studies also suggest that failure to disclose bad news is responsible for stock price crashes, which impose great wealth losses on investors (Kim et al., 2014; Kim & Zhang, 2016; Bao et al., 2018). Kim and Verrecchia (2001) model illustrates how a firm strategically manages its disclosure timing based on performance outcomes. The firm reports current period performance promptly when it falls within a predefined range, but defers disclosure if performance falls outside this range. The role of this model is to highlight how companies manage the flow of information to control market reactions, reduce negative impacts from poor performance, and influence investor perception. This approach reflects a strategic use of disclosure to mitigate the effects of performance volatility on stakeholder confidence. In a recent paper, Cheynel and Levine (2020) build a mosaic theory illustrating the conditions under which voluntary public disclosures may exacerbate information asymmetries rather than diminish them. It is also demonstrated that the beneficial capital market effects of additional disclosure depend on a credible commitment to maintaining that disclosure level (Baiman & Verrecchia, 1996; Leuz & Verrecchia, 2000).

Unlike voluntary disclosures, mandatory disclosures arise from two sources within the financial reporting environment: periodic reports that are a realization of ex ante reporting systems and event-driven mandatory filings-compliance (Bertomeu & Magee, 2015; Friedman et al., 2020; Gietzmann & Trombetta, 2003; Jorgensen & Kirschenheiter, 2003). Much of the literature on mandatory disclosure evaluates whether firms make disclosures because the benefits from exposure at the firm level are lower than the benefits for society. Regulators often mandate new disclosure requirements to improve information flow to society or to encourage a desired behavior (Coffee, 1984; Easterbrook & Fischel, 1984; Dye, 1990; Fox, 1999; Leuz & Wysocki, 2016). When managers communicate information about their firms, meaningfully affecting capital market outcomes, disclosure regulation under mandatory disclosure is frequently motivated by the desire to strengthen the market-wide information environment (Franke & Simons, 2023). Thus, evidence on market-wide effects could be more relevant (Leuz & Wysocki, 2016). By mandating firms to expand their financial reporting beyond their voluntary levels, regulating firms' financial reporting is expected to foster a more competitive and dispersed type of market-wide resource allocation (Zingales & Rajan, 2003). Mandatory financial reporting by firms reveals proprietary information to potential and existing competitors, increasing competition for proprietary information rents and potentially decreasing incentives to generate proprietary information.

However, mandatory disclosure also entails costs. One such cost concerns organizational learning: disclosures could reduce managers' ability to glean decision-relevant information from prices by discouraging informed trading (Jayaraman & Wu, 2019). Providing more public disclosure can crowd out other types of information (Breuer et al., 2022). This is particularly relevant in financial markets, where prices are thought to provide useful information to decision-makers. Goldstein and Yang (2019) argue that, paradoxically, disclosing more precise public information about the factor that the real decision-maker wants to learn can backfire as it interferes with the ability of the market to reveal this type of information, attenuating the positive direct effect of better disclosure. Many studies assume that firms' disclosures are "public" and that investors, thus, costlessly transform information from disclosures into prices.

Bank disclosures enrich a bank's information environment and allow regulators and external capital providers to monitor bank operations and risk-taking. Over the past decade, many researchers have focused on the most innovative aspects of disclosure in banking by considering the disclosures arising from stress testing required after the global financial crisis (Acharya et al., 2018). While stress tests likely increase the banking system's safety, there remains disagreement about the effects of disclosing the results of those stress tests to market participants. Theory tends to be pessimistic about the disclosure's potential to mitigate private information generation and dampen risk sharing. In contrast, empirical studies document more optimistic findings that suggest that testing disclosures may improve the overall information environment and encourage good risk-taking. One challenge in this literature is the difficulty of separating the effect of the underlying stress test from the disclosure effect. The 2023 bank failures invite further research to understand the effects of disclosing stress test results and verify the reliability of the reports' disclosure.

References

Acharya, V. V., Berger, A. N., & Roman, R. A. (2018). Lending implications of US bank stress tests: Costs or benefits? *Journal of Financial Intermediation, 34*, 58–90.

Armstrong, C. S., Guay, W. R., & Weber, J. P. (2010). The role of information and financial reporting in corporate governance and debt contracting. *Journal of Accounting and Economics, 50*(2–3), 179–234.

Baiman, S., & Verrecchia, R. E. (1996). The relation among capital markets, financial disclosure, production efficiency, and insider trading. *Journal of Accounting Research, 34*(1), 1–22.

Balakrishnan, K., Billings, M. B., Kelly, B., & Ljungqvist, A. (2014). Shaping liquidity: On the causal effects of voluntary disclosure. *Journal of Finance, 69*(5), 2237–2278.

Bao, D., Fung, S. Y. K., & Su, L. (2018). Can shareholders be at rest after adopting clawback provisions? Evidence from stock price crash risk. *Contemporary Accounting Research, 35*(3), 1578–1615.

Barth, M. E., & Landsman, W. R. (2010). How did financial reporting contribute to the financial crisis? *European Accounting Review, 19*(3), 399–423.

Berger, A. N., & Demirgüç-Kunt, A. (2021). Banking research in the time of COVID-19. *Journal of Financial Stability, 57*, 100939.

Berger, P. G. (2011). Challenges and opportunities in disclosure research—A discussion of 'the financial reporting environment: Review of the recent literature'. *Journal of Accounting and Economics, 51*(1–2), 204–218.

Bertomeu, J., & Magee, R. P. (2015). Mandatory disclosure and asymmetry in financial reporting. *Journal of Accounting and Economics, 59*(2–3), 284–299.

Beyer, A., Cohen, D. A., Lys, T. Z., & Walther, B. R. (2010). The financial reporting environment: Review of the recent literature. *Journal of Accounting and Economics, 50*(2–3), 296–343.

Bischof, J. (2009). The effects of IFRS 7 adoption on bank disclosure in Europe. *Accounting in Europe, 6*(2), 167–194.

Bischof, J., & Daske, H. (2013). Mandatory disclosure, voluntary disclosure, and stock market liquidity: Evidence from the EU bank stress tests. *Journal of Accounting Research, 51*(5), 997–1029.

Bischof, J., Daske, H., Elfers, F., & Hail, L. (2022). A tale of two supervisors: Compliance with risk disclosure regulation in the banking sector. *Contemporary Accounting Research, 39*(1), 498–536.

Bischof, J., Laux, C., & Leuz, C. (2021). Accounting for financial stability: Bank disclosure and loss recognition in the financial crisis. *Journal of Financial Economics, 141*(3), 1188–1217.

Boot, A. W., & Schmeits, A. (2000). Market discipline and incentive problems in conglomerate firms with banking applications. *Journal of Financial Intermediation, 9*(3), 240–273.

Bossone, B. (2001). Circuit theory of banking and finance. *Journal of Banking & Finance, 25*(5), 857–890.

Botosan, C. A. (1997). Disclosure level and the cost of equity capital. *Accounting Review*, 323–349.

Botosan, C. A., & Plumlee, M. A. (2002). A re-examination of disclosure level and the expected cost of equity capital. *Journal of Accounting Research, 40*(1), 21–40.

Breuer, M., Hombach, K., & Müller, M. A. (2022). When you talk, I remain silent: Spillover effects of peers' mandatory disclosures on firms' voluntary disclosures. *The Accounting Review, 97*(4), 155–186.

Bryant, J. (1980). A model of reserves, bank runs, and deposit insurance. *Journal of Banking & Finance, 4*(4), 335–344.

Bushman, R., & Landsman, W. R. (2010). The pros and cons of regulating corporate reporting: A critical review of the arguments. *Accounting and Business Research, 40*(3), 259–273.

Bushman, R. M. (2014). Thoughts on financial accounting and the banking industry. *Journal of Accounting and Economics, 58*(2–3), 384–395.

Bushman, R. M., & Williams, C. D. (2012). Accounting discretion, loan loss provisioning, and discipline of banks' risk-taking. *Journal of Accounting and Economics, 54*(1), 1–18.

Cheynel, E., & Levine, C. B. (2020). Public disclosures and information asymmetry: A theory of the mosaic. *The Accounting Review, 95*(1), 79–99.

Christensen, H. B., Floyd, E., Liu, L. Y., & Maffett, M. (2017). The real effects of mandated information on social responsibility in financial reports: Evidence from mine-safety records. *Journal of Accounting and Economics, 64*(2–3), 284–304.

Coffee, J. C., Jr. (1984). Market failure and the economic case for a mandatory disclosure system. *Virginia Law Review*, 717–753.

Coller, M., & Yohn, T. L. (1997). Management forecasts and information asymmetry: An examination of bid-ask spreads. *Journal of Accounting Research, 35*(2), 181–191.

Cordella, T., & Yeyati, E. L. (1998). Public disclosure and bank failures. *Staff Papers, 45*(1), 110–131.

Dang, T. V., Gorton, G., Holmstrom, B., & Ordonez, G. (2017). Banks as secret keepers. *The American Economic Review, 107*(4), 1005–1029.

Danisewicz, P., McGowan, D., Onali, E., & Schaeck, K. (2018). Debt priority structure, market discipline, and bank conduct. *The Review of Financial Studies, 31*(11), 4493–4555.

Degryse, H., Goncharenko, R., Theunisz, C., & Vadasz, T. (2021). The green transition and bank financing. *European Economy, 2*, 75–88.

Del Gaudio, B. L., Megaravalli, A. V., Sampagnaro, G., & Verdoliva, V. (2020). Mandatory disclosure tone and bank risk-taking: Evidence from Europe. *Economics Letters, 186*, 108531.

Diamond, D. W., & Dybvig, P. H. (1983). Bank runs, deposit insurance, and liquidity. *Journal of Political Economy, 91*(3), 401–419.

Dursun-de Neef, Ö., Forchieri, J., Gehrig, T., & Schandlbauer, A. (2023). How did banks' ESG conduct affect financial performance and lending during COVID-19?. *Available at SSRN.*

Dye, R. A. (1985). Disclosure of nonproprietary information. *Journal of Accounting Research*, 123–145.

Dye, R. A. (1990). Mandatory versus voluntary disclosures: The cases of financial and real externalities. *Accounting Review*, 1–24.

Dye, R. A. (2001). An evaluation of "essays on disclosure" and the disclosure literature in accounting. *Journal of Accounting and Economics, 32*(1–3), 181–235.

Easterbrook, F. H., & Fischel, D. R. (1984). Mandatory disclosure and the protection of investors. *Virginia Law Review*, 669–715.

Einhorn, E. (2005). The nature of the interaction between mandatory and voluntary disclosures. *Journal of Accounting Research, 43*(4), 593–621.

Eng, L. L., & Mak, Y. T. (2003). Corporate governance and voluntary disclosure. *Journal of Accounting and Public Policy, 22*(4), 325–345.

Flannery, M. J. (2020). Contrasting worldviews at bank and securities market regulators. *Journal of Money, Credit and Banking, 52*(S1), 43–62.

Flannery, M. J., Kwan, S. H., & Nimalendran, M. (2013). The 2007–2009 financial crisis and bank opaqueness. *Journal of Financial Intermediation, 22*(1), 55–84.

Fox, M. B. (1999). Retaining mandatory securities disclosure: Why issuer choice is not investor empowerment. *Virginia Law Review, 85*, 1335.

Franke, B., & Simons, D. (2023). Enforcement and disclosure. *Journal of Accounting and Public Policy, 42*(5), 107131.

Frankel, R., Jennings, J., & Lee, J. (2016). Using unstructured and qualitative disclosures to explain accruals. *Journal of Accounting and Economics, 62*(2–3), 209–227.

Freixas, X., & Rochet, J. C. (2008). *Microeconomics of banking*. MIT Press.

Friedman, H. L., Hughes, J. S., & Michaeli, B. (2020). Optimal reporting when additional information might arrive. *Journal of Accounting and Economics, 69*(2–3), 101276.

Giannetti, M., Jasova, M., Loumioti, M., & Mendicino, C. (2023). "Glossy Green" Banks: The Disconnect Between Environmental Disclosures and Lending Activities.

Gietzmann, M. B., & Trombetta, M. (2003). Disclosure interactions: Accounting policy choice and voluntary disclosure effects on the cost of raising outside capital. *Accounting and Business Research, 33*(3), 187–205.

Goldstein, I., & Yang, L. (2019). Good disclosure, bad disclosure. *Journal of Financial Economics, 131*(1), 118–138.

Gourdel, R., Monasterolo, I., Dunz, N., Mazzocchetti, A., & Parisi, L. (2022). The double materiality of climate physical and transition risks in the euro area.

Graham, J. R., Harvey, C. R., & Rajgopal, S. (2005). The economic implications of corporate financial reporting. *Journal of Accounting and Economics, 40*(1–3), 3–73.

Granja, J. (2013). The relation between bank resolutions and information environment: Evidence from the auctions for failed banks. *Journal of Accounting Research, 51*(5), 1031–1070.
Grossman, S. J. (1981). The informational role of warranties and private disclosure about product quality. *The Journal of Law and Economics, 24*(3), 461–483.
Grossman, S. J., & Hart, O. D. (1980). Takeover bids, the free-rider problem, and the theory of the corporation. *The Bell Journal of Economics*, 42–64.
Healy, P. M., & Palepu, K. G. (2001). Information asymmetry, corporate disclosure, and the capital markets: A review of the empirical disclosure literature. *Journal of Accounting and Economics, 31*(1–3), 405–440.
Holthausen, R. W. (2009). Accounting standards, financial reporting outcomes, and enforcement. *Journal of Accounting Research, 47*(2), 447–458.
Ibrahim, A. E. A., & Hussainey, K. (2019). Developing the narrative risk disclosure measurement. *International Review of Financial Analysis, 64*, 126–144.
Jayaraman, S., & Wu, J. S. (2019). Is silence golden? Real effects of mandatory disclosure. *The Review of Financial Studies, 32*(6), 2225–2259.
Jones, M., Melis, A., Gaia, S., & Aresu, S. (2018). Does graphical reporting improve risk disclosure? Evidence from European banks. *Journal of Applied Accounting Research, 19*(1), 161–180.
Jorgensen, B. N., & Kirschenheiter, M. T. (2003). Discretionary risk disclosures. *The Accounting Review, 78*(2), 449–469.
Kapan, T., & Minoiu, C. (2018). Balance sheet strength and bank lending: Evidence from the global financial crisis. *Journal of Banking & Finance, 92*, 35–50.
Kasznik, R., & Lev, B. (1995). To warn or not to warn: Management disclosures in the face of an earnings surprise. *Accounting Review*, 113–134.
Kim, C., & Zhang, L. (2016). Corporate political connections and tax aggressiveness. *Contemporary Accounting Research, 33*(1), 78–114.
Kim, O., & Verrecchia, R. E. (2001). The relation among disclosure, returns, and trading volume information. *The Accounting Review, 76*(4), 633–654.
Kim, S., Kumar, N., Lee, J., & Oh, J. (2023). ESG lending. In *Proceedings of Paris December 2021 Finance Meeting EUROFIDAI-ESSEC, European Corporate Governance Institute–Finance Working Paper* (No. 817).
Kim, Y., Li, H., & Li, S. (2014). Corporate social responsibility and stock price crash risk. *Journal of Banking & Finance, 43*, 1–13.
Kothari, S. P., Shu, S., & Wysocki, P. D. (2009). Do managers withhold bad news? *Journal of Accounting Research, 47*(1), 241–276.
Krinsky, I., & Lee, J. (1996). Earnings announcements and the components of the bid-ask spread. *The Journal of Finance, 51*(4), 1523–1535.
Laeven, L., & Levine, R. (2009). Bank governance, regulation and risk taking. *Journal of Financial Economics, 93*(2), 259–275.
Lamanda, G., & Tamasne Voneki, Z. (2020). What do risk disclosures reveal about banking operational risk processes? Content analysis of banks' risk disclosures in the Visegrad Four countries. *Journal of Operational Risk, 15*(1).
Landsman, W. R. (2007). Is fair value accounting information relevant and reliable? Evidence from capital market research. *Accounting and Business Research, 37*(supl), 19–30.
Leuz, C., & Verrecchia, R. E. (2000). The economic consequences of increased disclosure. *Journal of Accounting Research*, 91–124.
Leuz, C., & Wysocki, P. D. (2008). Economic consequences of financial reporting and disclosure regulation: A review and suggestions for future research. *Available at SSRN 1105398.*
Leuz, C., & Wysocki, P. D. (2016). The economics of disclosure and financial reporting regulation: Evidence and suggestions for future research. *Journal of Accounting Research, 54*(2), 525–622.
Lindblom, C. K. (1994). The implications of organizational legitimacy for corporate social performance and disclosure. In *Critical Perspectives on Accounting Conference, New York, 1994.*

Maffei, M., Aria, M., Fiondella, C., Spanò, R., & Zagaria, C. (2014). (Un) useful risk disclosure: Explanations from the Italian banks. *Managerial Auditing Journal, 29*(7), 621–648.
Mies, M. (2024). Bank opacity, systemic risk and financial stability. *Journal of Financial Stability, 70*, 101211.
Milgrom, P. R. (1981). Good news and bad news: Representation theorems and applications. *The Bell Journal of Economics*, 380–391.
Monasterolo, I., Billio, M., & Battiston, S. (2020). The importance of compound risk in the nexus of COVID-19, climate change and finance. *Climate Change and Finance (June 20, 2020).*
Morgan, D. P. (2002). Rating banks: Risk and uncertainty in an opaque industry. *American Economic Review, 92*(4), 874–888.
Nier, E. W. (2005). Bank stability and transparency. *Journal of Financial Stability, 1*(3), 342–354.
Scannella, E., & Polizzi, S. (2021). How to measure bank credit risk disclosure? Testing a new methodological approach based on the content analysis framework. *Journal of Banking Regulation, 22*, 73–95.
Schipper, K. (2007). Required disclosures in financial reports. *The Accounting Review, 82*(2), 301–326.
Shleifer, A. (2005). Understanding regulation. *European Financial Management, 11*(4), 439–451.
Skinner, D. J. (1994). Why firms voluntarily disclose bad news. *Journal of Accounting Research, 32*(1), 38–60.
Skinner, D. J. (1997). Earnings disclosures and stockholder lawsuits. *Journal of Accounting and Economics, 23*(3), 249–282.
Verrecchia, R. E. (1983). Discretionary disclosure. *Journal of Accounting and Economics, 5*, 179–194.
Verrecchia, R. E. (1990). Information quality and discretionary disclosure. *Journal of Accounting and Economics, 12*(4), 365–380.
Verrecchia, R. E. (2001). Essays on disclosure. *Journal of Accounting and Economics, 32*(1–3), 97–180.
Wang, L. L. (2023). Transmission effects of ESG disclosure regulations through bank lending networks. *Journal of Accounting Research, 61*(3), 935–978.
Zeghal, D., & Lahmar, Z. (2016). The impact of IFRS adoption on accounting conservatism in the European Union. *International Journal of Accounting and Financial Reporting, 6*(1), 127–160.
Zingales, L., & Rajan, R. (2003). Banks and markets: The changing character of European finance.

Chapter 2
Disclosure Regulation for Transparency, Stability, and Competition in Banking

2.1 The Economics of Disclosure Regulation

Disclosure regulation is fundamental for well-functioning banking markets. Regulators generally mandate new disclosure requirements to either improve the flow of information to a society or encourage a desired behavior. In this regard, the banking industry is no exception. In the aftermath of the financial crisis of 2007–2008, regulators have advocated for more stringent disclosure requirements for banks and other financial institutions. Policymakers have concluded that the financial crisis at that time resulted partly from insufficient disclosure. Banks were too opaque to recover from any financial diseases in the short run. Consequently, bank regulators and supervisory authorities promoted rules and recommendations that force financial entities to disclose more. A banking crisis represents a real threat to the economy: a bank crash leads to a dangerous contagion effect within and between banks and the rest of the economy and social welfare (Granja, 2013). Banks are strongly linked to the real sector and families' wealth by supporting them as first lenders. At the same time, banks like leveraging and tend to increase their risk-taking behavior anytime they can.

Today, policymakers advocate for disclosure regulations to ensure the smooth and stable functioning of banking and financial systems, mandating adherence to a diverse set of rules and standards:

- Banking rules (e.g., Basel frameworks)
- Accounting standards (e.g., International Financial Reporting Standards (IFRS) and Statement of Financial Accounting Standards (SFAS) frameworks)
- Supervisory rules required by central banks (e.g., European Central Bank (ECB), European Banking Authority (EBA), Federal Reserve (FED))
- Compliance rules required by other international entities (e.g., EU institutions, UN institutions, etc.)

© The Author(s), under exclusive license to Springer Nature Switzerland AG 2025
S. Longo, *Disclosure in Banking*, SIDREA Series in Accounting and Business Administration, https://doi.org/10.1007/978-3-031-84196-5_2

This regulatory architecture has given rise to a sense of overconfidence in having found the proper solution to prevent further financial crises—until the occurrence of two notable bank failures in March 2023 (e.g., Silicon Valley Bank and Credit Suisse). These recent banking crashes destroyed this belief and emphasized the need to properly disclose risks for a more accurate valuation of banks' risk profiles (Bischof et al., 2021). Bank disclosure involves providing financial and risk information to allow the monitoring of senior management's behavior, reduce uncertainty about a firm's expected future cash flows, and support banks' legitimacy and reputation. Suppose there is a conviction that the lesson of the 2007–2008 financial crisis has been learned. In that sense, the financial banking cases of March 2023 have demonstrated that disclosure regulation cannot be considered a final, evergreen solution to any problem. Undoubtedly, disclosure regulation can provide several benefits for capital market participants, but it cannot be viewed as a solution to all problems to avoid future crises or frauds.

Disclosure regulations are frequently motivated by the desire to strengthen the market-wide information environment. Particularly, regulators require firms to provide better disclosure to their investors, addressing problems in credit-rating agencies to make credit ratings a more precise and reliable source of public information. Providing information seems desirable as we want decision-makers to make more informed and efficient decisions. Suppose we imagine a world without disclosure regulation. In that case, a firm decides on its disclosure by weighing benefits, such as reduced adverse selection discounts, against costs, such as proprietary information loss. This firm could consider peer firms' disclosure decisions that are relevant for stakeholders. Shifting to a mandatory regime, disclosure requirements push the regulated firm's disclosure above its level in a voluntary regime (disclosure game—Admati & Pfleiderer, 2000; Breuer et al., 2022). Consequently, the unregulated firm reduces its disclosure below its level in a voluntary regime. First, greater disclosure by peers reduces stakeholders' uncertainty about the firm and, hence, the firm's benefit from its disclosure. Second, the regulated peer firm cannot react to the unregulated firm's reduction of its disclosure because the regulated firm's best response function is constrained from below. The result is an equilibrium in which the unregulated firm can reduce its own disclosure and proprietary costs without suffering from an increase in its stakeholders' uncertainty. Stakeholders' uncertainty does not increase because the regulated firm cannot respond by reducing its disclosure when the unregulated firm reduces disclosure.

The demand for financial disclosure, particularly reporting, stems from information asymmetry and agency conflicts between managers and outside investors. The credibility of management disclosures is bolstered by the involvement of regulators, standard setters, auditors, and other capital market intermediaries. However, it is important to recognize that we operate in a world with multiple sources of information asymmetry. Regulation restricting disclosure related to one source of asymmetric information may inadvertently reduce rather than improve welfare (Allen & Carletti, 2008; Plantin et al., 2008). This is because restrictions on disclosures related to one activity may have unintended consequences concerning the (possibly unregulated) disclosures related to other sources of asymmetric information

(Kanodia et al., 2005). Disclosure regulation affects the disclosure frequency and, consequently, both managerial and investor behaviors (Ernstberger et al., 2017). Thus, it is more effective only when monitoring compliance is regularly enforced by efficient institutions (Healy & Palepu, 2001). The use of regulation as an enforcement mechanism to monitor compliance and impose punishments in cases of non-compliance enhances compliance levels. Banks only comply with mandatory requirements if stringent regulation is in place. Regulation is stringent "if it allows only one outcome, has an adequate enforcement mechanism, and sanctions for non-compliance." Nevertheless, disclosure regulation requires banks to provide comprehensive disclosure. For instance, banking technology has dramatically reduced the information costs between banks and investors, depositors, and borrowers, facilitating information collection that was unthinkable just one century ago.

2.2 Disclosure Regulation for Market Discipline

The numerous policy initiatives enhance the importance of market discipline in safeguarding banking financial stability and soundness. For instance, IFRS-IAS, Basel agreements, and other regulatory initiatives are dedicated to increasing transparency and stability. But how can regulation contribute to market discipline? The answer is that banks should release enough information about their operations so that market participants can make informed assessments of their financial condition. The concept of market discipline, as applied to banks and financial institutions, focuses on the financial firm's security holders as the market agents involved in disciplining the firm. The potential for market discipline to complement or serve as a substitute for bank supervision and regulation has long been recognized (Gilbert, 1990). Indeed, the corporate governance literature suggests that in most industries, investors are well placed to control or influence borrower behavior in primary markets. However, distortions of market-based governance incentives by government guarantees or regulatory mechanisms can weaken the ability of investors to discipline firms. Even if investors have full information and market signals are clear to all participants, markets will fail to discipline banks if government policies insulate managers from market signals. For example, Distinguin et al. (2006) test whether accounting data and equity markets assist in predicting distress for European banks. They find that market-based indicators have predictive power for assessing the degree of bank stress, but only for banks that rely less heavily on insured deposits. In contrast, examinations (like regulatory stress tests) provide new information that market prices do not immediately reflect, indicating that regulation may uncover information more readily than markets for bank debts. DeYoung and Roland (2001) suggest that regulators are more likely to uncover "bad" private information. They also find that new information uncovered by supervisory examinations influences bank values. They argue that when information obtained by supervisory examinations is released, market prices reflect the information and likely regulatory actions. Billett et al. (1995) provide an analysis suggesting that regulatory actions responding to new information about risks give imperfectly competitive banks incentives to reshuffle liabilities to protect themselves from market discipline. The question is whether regulators should release all the information gathered during the examinations to compensate for missing information unavailable to market players. The combination of mandated information disclosure and market mechanisms makes it harder to disentangle the effects of regulatory stances and practices on market discipline. Nevertheless, despite the information environment results being crowded, bond and equity investors can respond well enough to available information about banks' risk characteristics to induce movements in rates of return (Jordan et al., 2000). Evidence also suggests that banks have the discretion to withhold certain information or make income statements or balance sheet adjustments that influence the information content of their disclosures (Landsman, 2006). In any case, a greater degree of information disclosure is associated with a less fragile banking system.

2.3 Disclosure Regulation for Transparency

Regulatory activities encompass compliance with disclosure rules designed to ensure bank transparency. Bank transparency means the availability to outside stakeholders of relevant, reliable information about the periodic performance, financial position, business model, governance, and risks of banks (Bushman, 2014). Thus, regulators promote transparency, requiring firms to increase the quality of financial accounting. Due to their business model as financial intermediaries, banks are generally seen as opaque, which has negative consequences for overall financial market stability (Morgan, 2002). The lack of disclosure increases uncertainty. Consequently, more transparency is required to monitor the risks associated with using financial instruments. Barth and Schipper (2008) "define financial reporting transparency as the extent to which financial reports reveal an entity's underlying economics in a way that is readily understandable by those using the financial reports." There is a broader agreement that lack of transparency facilitated fraudulent activities during certain periods, ultimately contributing to the 2007–2008 financial crisis, one of the most significant in history.consensus to admit that opacity. In cases like these, investors and regulators often discover pertinent information too late to be able to take measures to prevent a potential crisis from happening.

However, it is not automatic that regulated disclosure increases transparency. Thus, regulators require mandatory disclosure to maintain an information environment that guarantees transparency for investors and other stakeholders, including citizens. Banks like to play around with transparency thresholds, managing their transparency level in a way that affects economic activity and growth. Generally, transparency allows for the reduction of adverse selection concerns and uncertainty when new financial and economic turbulences arise. Moreover, it improves economic efficiency by discouraging investments and innovations, as banking risk exposing proprietary information to business partners (e.g., customers and suppliers) and competitors. When a bank determines its level of transparency, it does so by weighing the trade-off between the private benefits and costs associated with revealing information. Firms with high external financing needs tend to employ high levels of transparency, allowing them to obtain competitive funding from a dispersed set of capital providers. In contrast, firms with high proprietary costs tend to adopt lower levels of transparency.

Firms are required to disclose mandatorily to instill investor confidence in public capital markets. Today, in many countries worldwide, mandatory disclosure aims to protect the interests of various stakeholders. Furthermore, mandated disclosure can affect industry-wide resource allocation. By mandating accurate public reporting, the emphasis on close relationships for resource allocation is reduced, allowing banks to broaden their ownership base through increased transparency. From a market perspective, mandatory disclosure can facilitate the entry of new players, increasing competition (Breuer, 2021). However, a question arises about how new firms, like financial start-ups, can benefit from these mandates if they are affected by disclosure regulations. They could be excluded from these requirements due to their size, without systematically impacting the rest of the banking-financial industry, thereby gaining competitive advantages. Conversely, these mandates could indirectly affect them since they are connected with big sharks (i.e., banking conglomerates), potentially allowing them to avoid a form of market competition. Finally, they could fall into the category of a shadow banking system, which operates outside of any regulatory or supervisory controls, which sometimes represents a real risk for the entire banking system (Bakk-Simon et al., 2012).

Returning to the fundamental importance of mandatory disclosure for transparency, we see that disclosure regulation is always applied to specific parties rather than to the entire market. In the accounting and finance literature, many efforts have been made to measure the effects of mandatory disclosure. Many regulatory initiatives have been considered, leading to contrasting and, for this reason, nongeneralizable results. In economics, the effects—or, rather, the real effects—of mandatory disclosure are measured broadly from an investor's perspective. Disclosure matters, but today, it has become very challenging to understand how mandatory disclosure can respond to the need for more transparency for investors and many other stakeholders based on an unsophisticated regulatory architecture. Not everyone seems satisfied in terms of transparency in the short run. Still, in the long run, mandatory disclosure can modify economic behaviors at the firm and managerial levels. In this way, the effects of mandatory disclosure can be assessed according to expectations, allowing for a more transparent environment overall.

2.4 Transparency in Assessing Financial Stability

Whether transparency helps or hurts the financial system's stability is an unresolved question (Nier, 2005; Tadesse, 2006; Novotny-Farkas, 2016). A large body of theoretical literature explores bank transparency by understanding how it affects the risk profile of individual banks and the financial system. On the one hand, informational asymmetry and the positive externality explanations of regulated disclosure predict that disclosure and the consequent transparency enhance banking system stability by enabling market participants to better assess bank risk and performance ("transparency-stability" view). On the other hand, regulated disclosure could exacerbate banking system instability by creating negative informational externalities ("transparency-fragility" view). Overall, this literature finds that while credible public information about individual banks can enhance the ability of regulators and market participants to monitor banks' behavior and discipline them, there are also endogenous costs associated with transparency that can be detrimental to the banking system.

From a positive and conservative perspective, high-quality financial reporting is a key success factor for effective market discipline and regulation in banking (Acharya & Ryan, 2016). Accounting regulation has played an essential role in addressing past financial crises. With more stringent financial accounting requirements, risk disclosure could help investors, depositors, and many other market players distinguish healthy from unhealthy banks (Novotny-Farkas, 2016). The same supervisors could benefit from risk disclosure to understand timeliness and accurately assess a bank's risk exposure, in addition to reducing the cost of capital (Poshakwale & Courtis, 2005; Fiechter & Zhou, 2016; Heinle & Smith, 2017), increasing market liquidity (Bischof & Daske, 2013), and improving bank valuation (Elbannan & Elbannan, 2015; Giner et al., 2020). Jungherr (2018) studies the relationship between bank opacity and financial crises and demonstrates, through a model, how transparency affects bank value and social welfare:

1) Market discipline is based on transparency's capacity to lower risk-taking. A transparent bank, anticipating its publicly observed portfolio choice, would influence creditors' beliefs about the value of its assets by choosing a (more possible) safe portfolio to reduce the risk of a bank run. In contrast, opacity does not have the power to affect creditors' beliefs. This increases the incentive to pick a risky portfolio.
2) The Hirshleifer effect (where Hirshleifer (1971) provides an early example of how public information reduces risk-sharing opportunities among agents) is grounded on the fact that transparency may increase the incidence of bank runs for a given level of risk-taking. If banks' risk exposure is unobservable, outsiders cannot distinguish weak banks from strong ones. Transparency destroys this pooling mechanism and exposes weak banks to bank runs (Dang et al., 2017).
3) The spillover effect is caused by a transparent portfolio that reveals a bank's private information. The bank's competitors benefit as additional information helps them select a better portfolio.

At the time of this study, further empirical research has focused on evidence for bank transparency, starting from the problems created by its opposite concept—opacity. Fosu et al. (2017) analyze the impact of opacity on financial stability by evaluating the risk behavior of US banks from 1995 to 2013. They find that opacity increases the risk of bankruptcy for credit institutions. Gallemore (2023), using a sample of US commercial banks during the 2007–2009 financial crisis, argues that banks' financial reporting opacity, measured by delayed expected loan loss recognition, hurts the intervention decisions made by bank regulators. Mies (2024) examines the impact of bank opacity on European financial stability, considering the role of risk disclosure regulation. Based on a panel dataset of listed European banks covering 2002–2018, he finds that bank opacity significantly influences institution-specific contribution to the âˆ†conditional value at risk and marginal expected shortfall. Therefore, the enforcement mechanism and the policies introduced by accounting standard setters and regulators for the risk disclosure of banks positively impact the reduction of systemic risks. And the banking regulator seems more effective in requiring compliance with risk disclosure (Bischof et al., 2022). The effects are stronger if the central bank is responsible for bank supervision.

2.5 Toward Competition in Banking Markets

A further question is whether transparency brings the same positive effects to bank stability and contemporary competition. Like other firms of different sectors, banks must attract outside funding in competitive capital markets, face competition in product and labor markets, and deal with corporate governance issues arising from managerial self-interest and asymmetric information. Bushman et al. (2015) and Dou et al. (2014) find that the extent to which banks delay loan loss recognition increases as the competition a bank faces intensifies. These papers exploit the process of bank deregulation to identify exogenous changes in bank competition. Differently, accounting policy choices that delay expected loss recognition can heighten capital adequacy concerns during crisis periods. Indeed, an inadequate capital level leads to a decreasing survival probability, competitive position, and market share (Berger & Bouwman, 2013). Therefore, achieving a transparency equilibrium at the bank level becomes challenging and complex. For example, if a bank reveals its own portfolio choice, rival banks can infer the underlying private information, which allows them to select a better portfolio. This increases the expected return that rival banks can offer households at the expense of the transparent bank's market share. Information spillover, therefore, represents a private cost for competing banks. A bank's portfolio choice is proprietary information. Competing banks act as in a prisoner's dilemma: each of them reduces its level of transparency to avoid revealing private information to its rivals. The associated reduction in market discipline leads banks to take on too much risk. And this is inefficient. In this sense, policymakers can improve the market outcome by imposing public disclosure requirements. Jones et al. (2013) examine the impact of opacity on the profitability and valuation of banks during the period 2000–2007, noting that investing in opaque assets leads to higher required returns and, consequently, higher valuation discounts compared with transparent assets. However, the following increase in systematic risks among banks, accompanied by a decrease in investments in transparent assets, increases the severity of the consequences postcrisis. In conclusion, full transparency generally maximizes neither efficiency nor stability.

Darrough (1993) argues that greater transparency can increase competition by revealing some strategic information, thus decreasing competitive advantage. Leuz and Wysocki (2016) highlight that disclosure costs can impede the functioning of smaller institutions compared to larger ones due to the effects of economies of scale, with a consequent decline in competition. Mandatory disclosure through transparency has the power to overcome market barriers, making it easier for new entrants to operate in the market. Mandatory disclosure plays a fundamental role against information asymmetry because it enhances the quality of information with real effects on reducing the cost of capital and increasing market liquidity. Nevertheless, managerial strategies could lead to different outcomes by balancing transparency and competition. Managers can decrease transparency to increase competition without revealing their competitive advantage. Every time we consider the banking industry, the story becomes more complicated because of the high degree of information asymmetry associated with bank risks. I started considering the literature on transparency for competition, which suggests that greater disclosure improves social welfare, market discipline, and financial stability and reduces corruption (Bauman & Nier, 2003; Nier, 2005; Barth et al., 2009). Mandatory disclosure to depositors or deposit insurance agencies forces banks to switch from price competition to asset quality competition (Cordella & Yeyati, 2002). This, in turn, leads to higher profits in the short term and to a greater number of players in the long term. Such a situation can be explained by the fact that risk is a cost in a bank's profit maximization problem. When a bank improves the quality of its assets, the deposit rate is reduced, which in the short term leads to higher expected bank profits. Nevertheless, higher transparency can lead to a higher probability of bank runs. But again, it depends on the starting level of bank transparency. If most banks are exposed to detailed disclosure, this could reduce competition, as stable banks might gain increased market power. Studies by Morris and Shin (2002) and Chen and Hasan (2006) show that greater transparency can lead to overreaction to potentially misleading public signals. Similarly, Moreno and Takalo (2016) argue that beyond a certain level, transparency negatively impacts total welfare (as measured by the the creditors' ex ante expected payoffs in their model). Landier and Thesmar (2011) suggest that excessive transparency can reduce social welfare, as complex financial information tends to be understood only by a small group of sophisticated agents.

Banks are among the most heavily regulated and supervised institutions on the planet. In addition to enforcing antitrust rules specially tailored to the banking industry, over the years, governments have implemented a wide range of regulatory policies, including restrictions on market entry, exit, and branching; explicit limits on bank loan and deposit rates; and a variety of rules governing the structure of banks' balance sheets. Andrievskaya and Semenova (2016) find that banking markets are less concentrated in countries with stricter disclosure requirements. This effect increases with the growth of bank credit risks. Nevertheless, when these risks are too high, regulation concerning information disclosure becomes less effective and can lead to opposite results. Moreover, unlike the regulator's expectations, market power is higher in countries with higher disclosure standards. However, this result is not stable and depends on model specification. Then disclosure requirements are more effective in developing countries than in developed ones. This is possibly due to the relatively low level of regulation in these countries. Therefore, the marginal effect of additional regulation in developing countries is higher than in developed countries.

2.6 Bridging Transparency, Financial Stability, and Competition

Prior studies examine the determinants of competition in the financial sector, the effect of competition on financial stability, the relationship between transparency and the efficiency of the banking system, and the possible effect of banking system transparency on bank competition. Regulators sometimes assume that greater banking system transparency should be practiced to influence the level of competition. Goetz (2018) finds that competition increases stability, improving bank profitability and asset quality. However, in an environment with greater competition, the pressure on profits will make banks choose riskier portfolios, leading to greater fragility (Hellmann et al., 2000). Thus, too much competition may lead to excessive risk-taking as it reduces margins (Marcus, 1984; Keeley, 1990; Allen & Gale, 2004). Contrary to this, we also see that banks earn lower rents in a more competitive environment, reducing their monitoring incentives (Allen & Gale, 2000). Focusing on bank concentration and bank market power, where large and small banks characterize the banking market, size can make a difference during economic growth and crisis (Berger et al., 2017). It is particularly observable that when borrowing financial constraints increase (indicating a period of economic crisis—see Ruckes, 2004), small banks, compared to large banks, are much more competitive because they use soft information and borrower-lender communication is much easier (Berger & Udell, 2002; Berger et al., 2005). On the other hand, large banks have the power to diversify risks so that banking systems dominated by a few large banks are likely to be less fragile than banking systems with many small banks (Allen & Gale, 2004). Finally, some hold that a few large banks are easier to monitor and supervise compared to competitive banking systems with many small banks (Beck et al., 2003). These arguments are all consistent with competition leading to greater fragility. Higher competition leads banks to assume more risks and diversify risks. This effect is also important for the banking system, especially in countries with weak supervision and private monitoring, government ownership, and public policies restricting competition. Bank competition does not depend on the transparency level per se, but it also relies on the geographical distance from the headquartered country. Distance does not help banks maintain the same level of transparency gained in the home country. Toh and Jia (2021) suggest that foreign banks from countries with cultural, economic, and institutional distance from the host country encounter difficulty in adapting to the local environment and exercising their existing competitive advantages in the host country. Their findings point to evidence of the "home-field advantage" of domestic banks, as they possess a greater ability to withstand interest margins. In contrast, foreign banks lose their competitive advantage because of distance and lower transparency.

In conclusion, the impact of transparency on a bank's financial stability and competition is not one-dimensional, as the arguments on the matter are conflicting. It took about 50 years to understand how the loss of bank credit supply resulting from bank failures during the crisis made the Great Depression much worse (Bernanke, 1983). There is still much room to investigate the interrelation between transparency, stability, and competition to better address policymakers' efforts.

2.7 How to Measure Banking Disclosure: A Set of Proxies

There seems to be a consensus among regulators and scholars that it is necessary to raise the level of bank information disclosure to improve the functioning of a banking system. Indeed, a key source of bank transparency is publicly disclosed financial reports that provide bank-specific information to investors and regulators seeking to understand banks' fundamentals to guide them in their investment decisions, manage their risk-taking, and enhance stability (Bushman & Williams, 2015). Providing more highly transparent or better-quality financial statements could increase publicly available information about banks' risk exposure and overall economic condition (Acharya & Ryan, 2016). Understanding how to measure transparency has represented a crucial point in academic literature, particularly bank transparency, given the complexity of the banking sector. Thus, previous empirical studies have used various proxies for bank transparency, including both accounting measures and custom-built indexes, as alternative approaches:

I. The timely recognition of expected loan losses incorporated in banks' *loan loss provisions* (LLPs), following Beatty and Liao (2011) and Bushman and Williams (2012): LLPs are broadly regarded as a standard channel through which the information quality of banks' financial reporting is evaluated as to how accurately the risk attributes of loan portfolios are reflected. Since the assessment of future loan losses involves significant subjectivity, a wide range of discretion is typically given to banks in determining their adequate levels of LLPs. Accordingly, when banks delay the recognition of expected losses, they may conceal the risk attributes of loan portfolios from outsiders, and the unrecognized amount of risk can create future loss overhangs (Bushman & Williams, 2012; Andries et al., 2017).
II. *Discretionary or abnormal loan loss provisions* (ALLPs) may reflect banks' opportunistic earnings or capital management motives. If banks use more discretion in providing loan losses to manage their earnings or regulatory capital, it will obscure the banks' fundamentals and reduce the quality of disclosed information (Dal Maso et al., 2018; Kim et al., 2020).

III. Following Chen et al. (2022), the adjusted R-squared (Adj. R^2) for each bank-quarter is derived from the regression $WriteOff_{(t,\,t+1)} = \alpha_0 + \sum_{j=1}^{2} \gamma_j LLP_{(t-j)} + \sum_{j=1}^{2} \beta_j EBLLP_{(t-j)} + \rho \Delta NPL_{(t-1)} + \delta Capital_{(t-1)} + \varepsilon_t$, estimated using the bank's observations from quarter t to quarter $t-1$, where LLP is the loan loss provision, EBLLP is the earnings before the loan loss provision at the beginning of quarter t, ΔNPL is the change in nonperforming loans in quarter $t - 1$ from quarter t, capital is shareholders' equity divided by total assets. A low R^2 does not necessarily imply that banks are riskier. This is because R^2 measures the proportion of uncertainty that depositors can resolve about banks' future loan portfolio performance.

IV. *Firms' share liquidity*: in theory, the link between transparency and market liquidity arises from reduced adverse selection (associated with information asymmetries between potential buyers and sellers of firm shares) through enhanced firm disclosure (Verrecchia, 2001). Many empirical studies support the notion of a positive relationship between a firm's disclosure level and the liquidity of its shares (Welker, 1995; Healy et al., 1999; Leuz & Verrecchia, 2000; Daske et al., 2008). Recent evidence suggests that this relationship is even more pronounced in times of financial crisis (Lang et al., 2012).

V. *Disclosure* as a dummy variable equal to 1 to indicate when a bank starts disclosing information and 0 otherwise (Semenova, 2012; Bischof & Daske, 2013; Bischof et al., 2023): this is in line with the commonly used measures of binary indicators of whether a firm publicly provides an annual report, files a 10-K or other disclosure forms with the Securities and Exchange Commission (SEC), reports financial statements quarterly, reports under IFRS, US generally accepted accounting principles (GAAP), or a particular reporting regime. Similarly, studies use variables characterizing disclosure policies, for example, whether and how frequently a firm provides management forecasts, hosts conference calls, issues press releases, etc. Generally, these variables are focused on the existence of a certain disclosure (policy).

VI. *Natural logarithm of the bid-ask spread* (Glosten & Milgrom, 1985; Daske et al., 2008; Muller et al., 2011; Stenfors, 2018): prior literature suggests using the mean quoted spread by starting in month â^'5 and ending in month +7 relative to the bank's fiscal year-end (Leuz & Verrecchia, 2000; Leuz, 2003). Transaction costs should be lower in large and liquid markets (and bid-ask spreads tighter). The bid-ask spread can be seen as a proxy for market liquidity, ultimately determined by the competitive market's trading volume, turnover, and volatility. Conversely, bid-ask spreads tend to widen with trading activity, order size, and quoting frequency, which are linked to greater uncertainty.

VII. *Earnings quality* (Kanagaretnam et al., 2014; Manganaris et al., 2017): transparency and accountability are essential for investors and other stakeholders because high earnings quality provides information about the features of a firm's financial performance relevant to a specific decision made by a specific decision-maker (Dechow et al., 2010). Earnings quality refers to the stability and persistence of reported earnings, the use of reported earnings to predict future cash flow, and the ability to reflect a company's true earnings.

VIII. *Standard deviation of earnings per share* (EPS) *forecasts*: the greater the number of analysts, the more information is available for investors and, therefore, the more transparent the banks. In addition, with greater transparency, there should be less dispersion in analysts' forecasts of EPS. Thus, larger forecast dispersion is associated with less transparent banks (Akhigbe et al., 2013).

IX. A combination of several measures—four transparency measures (*return volatility*, *volume*, *forecast error*, and *number of analysts* (Akhigbe et al., 2017)): theory suggests that transparency and volatility are inversely related (Madhavan, 1995). Importantly, Baumann and Nier (2005) conclude that banks that disclose more information and are more transparent exhibit lower stock price volatility.

X. *Disclosure/transparency index* (Andrievskaya & Semenova, 2016), an index based on the World Bank Banking Regulation and Supervision Survey questions related to bank disclosure and transparency: (1) Are off-balance sheet items disclosed to the public? (2) Must banks disclose their risk management procedures to the public? (3) Are bank directors legally liable if the information disclosed is erroneous or misleading? (4) Is an outside-licensed audit obligatory for a bank? A positive answer for each question receives 1 point, and a negative one receives 0 point. Therefore, the index's maximum level is 4.

XI. *Disclosure intensity index* is based on five aspects of corporate reporting: (1) financial disclosure intensity, (2) governance disclosure intensity, (3) accounting principles used to measure financial disclosures, (4) timeliness of financial disclosures, and (5) audit quality of financial disclosures (Bushman et al., 2004). The source of these variables is the International Accounting and Auditing Trends of the Center for Financial Analysis and Research (CIFAR) (1995).

XII. *Disclosure informativeness index* measures the degree to which bank disclosure accurately represents the financial conditions of banks. For example, reporting interest income from nonperforming loans as part of bank income overstates the true economic performance of the bank, as does the selective reporting of bank activities. Disclosure informativeness is measured by aggregating whether nonperforming loans are accurately presented and whether banks must present their bank and nonbank activities in a consolidated financial statement.

XIII. *Disclosure timeliness index* measures the degree to which bank disclosure is close to the decision timepoint of potential information users. This is a function of the frequency with which information is available to users. Bushman et al. (2004).

XIV. *Disclosure credibility* measures the degree to which bank-generated disclosure is subject to verification by an external audit that is independent, professional, and rigorous, as reflected by the regulations that govern bank auditing practices. Specifically, it measures the stringency of external audits in terms of whether they are compulsory, whether the scope of external audits is mandated, whether there is a license requirement for auditors, and whether auditors have independence in reporting to supervisory bodies. The variable is a principal component of the following five indicator variables:

(i) A variable that takes the value of 1 if the external audit of banks is compulsory in the country
(ii) A variable that takes 1 if there are specific regulatory requirements for the extent of the audit
(iii) A variable that takes 1 if auditors are required to be licensed or certified
(iv) A variable that takes 1 if auditors' report should be given to a supervisory agency, and
(v) A variable that takes 1 if supervisors can meet external auditors to discuss audit reports without bank approval

XV. *Index measuring the extent and comprehensiveness of financial reporting required of banks* (Tadesse, 2006)—its values are the principal component of four indicator variables:

(i) Presentation of nonperforming loans—a variable that takes 1 if bank regulation requires that accrued income on nonperforming loans should not be reported
(ii) Reporting consolidated financial statements—a variable that takes 1 if consolidated financial statements of bank and nonbank subsidiaries are required
(iii) Reporting off-balance sheet to the public—a variable that takes 1 if off-balance sheet items are required to be disclosed to the public
(iv) Reporting risk management practice—a variable that takes 1 if banks must disclose risk management practices to the public

XVI. *A further disclosure index* measures bank transparency by constructing three categories of measures based on the following;

(1) The management discussion and analysis (MD&A) section of annual reports (i.e., 10-K filings)
(2) The voluntary items in 8- K filings
(3) Forward-looking earnings guidance provided by the bank's managers (Jiang et al., 2022)

XVII. *Another index* for bank transparency has been constructed using cross-country data on bank regulatory provisions that regulate local disclosure practices by banks. Data are obtained from the database on bank supervision and regulation maintained by the World Bank (Barth et al., 2001a, 2001b). The database is constructed based on surveys of national bank regulatory and supervisory authorities in 1998 and 1999. The data from the survey have been extensively used in recent bank regulation studies (e.g., Barth et al., 2004; Beck et al., 2003; Cull et al., 2005; Claessens & Laeven, 2004; Demirgüç-Kunt & Detragiache, 2005; Tadesse, 2006).

At this stage, it is necessary to recall the importance of central banks' transparency. Today, central banks around the world are responsible not only for the monetary policies they adopt but also, increasingly, for safeguarding financial stability. Researchers like Horváth and Vaško (2016) propose the newly constructed financial stability-transparency (FST) index for 110 countries from 2000 to 2011.

XVIII. The financial stability-transparency index is the sum of the following 11 items (the number of points granted for each category is indicated in parentheses):

1. The goal of financial stability is explicitly stated in the central bank act (0—not stated, 1—explicitly stated).
2. The publication of the FSR (0—not published, 1—published).
3. The publication of the FSR—frequency (0—not published, 1/2—published annually, 1—published semi-annually or more often).
4. The FSR is forward-looking (0—not forward-looking, 1—includes outlooks and forecasts of risks).
5. The coverage of the FSR (in total, a max. of 1.5 points). (a) Macroeconomic environment and its risks (1/2 if included). (b) Deposit takers information and its risks (1/2 if included). (c) Other subjects or market information and risks (1/2 if included).
6. The publication of stress test (0—stress test not published, 1/2 published annually, 1—published more often).
7. The publication of FSIs (0—not published, 1/2—the core set of FSIs published, 1—both core and encouraged set published).
8. Macroprudential policy transparency (0—not described, 1/2—general strategy and cooperation described, 1—detailed policy and crisis management described).
9. The existence of a financial stability policy committee (0—no committee, 1—committee with regular meetings and clear strategy).
10. A separate section on financial stability on the central bank's website (0—no separate page (section) on the web, 1—separate page on the web).
11. A separate section (database) on the central bank's website for speeches about financial stability (0—no separate section, 1/2 separate section).

Researchers have also identified bank transparency through alternative disclosure methods, as regulators and supervisors require.

XIX. *Regulatory enforcement of financial reporting transparency* is identified in the likelihood of regulatory restatements (Costello et al., 2019). A restatement captures how the regulator takes action to correct accounting mistakes, errors, and irregularities that misstate reported capital. A greater incidence of regulatory restatements enhances the accuracy and reliability of financial reports, thereby improving the bank's transparency (Goldstein & Sapra, 2014; Parlatore, 2015).

In conclusion, bank transparency was particularly reached after the 2008 financial crisis. Researchers have tried to identify it in several ways. Today, an increase in transparency is possible through disclosure regulation. Thus, disclosure can be required by regulators and also supervisors. New regulations and supervision technicalities have emerged in the aftermath of the 2007–2008 crisis, including accounting (IFRS 9) and banking (Basel III Framework) rules and the new further periodic stress tests for the largest financial institutions. Criticism and concerns have arisen regarding this new regulatory architecture. For instance, Fed Chairman Ben Bernanke cautioned, "When the stress assessment was starting, some observers had warned that the assessment and, in particular, the public disclosure of the results might backfire." However, after the recent failures of banks (Credit Suisse and Silicon Valley Bank) in 2023, there is now a conviction to improve the coordination of rules to make information accurate, reliable, and readable in the eyes of investors and other market participants. This requires collaboration between regulators (accounting standard setters and banking regulators) and supervisors (central banks) to ensure that banks, ex ante and ex post, fairly adopt and respect the rules. The two recent bank failures have prompted further reflection on the importance of transparency for stability, regardless of the size of the bank. A revisitation of this topic is proposed in the next chapter.

Bank "opacity" and "transparency" represent two sides of the same coin. Empirical studies propose several identification strategies to examine the relationship between bank opacity and financial stability (see Table 2.1). Financial stability has been evaluated using idiosyncratic default risk measures, such as Z-score (Cao & Juelsrud, 2022; Fosu et al., 2017; Tran et al., 2022) and distance-to-default (Vallascas & Keasey, 2013) or stock price risk (Dewally & Shao, 2013; Hagendorff et al., 2013). Mies (2024) seeks to address this gap by examining the direct impact of opacity on systemic risk measures. According to regulation (EU No. 1093/2010), systemic risk is defined as the "risk of disruption in the financial system that could have serious negative consequences for the internal market and the real economy."

Furthermore, accounting and banking research is based mostly on European banks' experience (Mies, 2024; Longo et al., 2024). European capital markets have had a uniform regulatory and supervisory framework for bank transparency since 2014 due to the Capital Requirements Regulation (EU) No. 575/2013 (CRR), the Capital Requirements Directive 2013/36/EU (CRD), and the Single Supervisory Mechanism (SSM). In particular, the Basel 3 requirements of the Basel Committee have been codified into European law as a supranational regulatory framework—the CRD-IV package—which is mandatory for all EU member states. For instance, Longo et al. (2024) document a negative market reaction to the announcements of CRD IV rules on a sample of 145 listed European banks, indicating that transparency increases are borne by shareholders, with detrimental impacts on bank stock

Table 2.1 Overview of prior banking literature's opacity and risk proxies

Proxy for opacity	Proxy for financial stability	Author(s) – year
Interest rate derivatives reported to total assets (HI)	Crash as a dummy that is equal to 1 if a bank experiences one crash during the year and 0 otherwise Negative conditional return skewness of weekly bank-specific return (NCSKEW) Natural logarithm of the ratio of the standard deviation on the down weeks to the standard deviation on the up weeks (DUVOL)	Dewally and Shao (2013)
The absolute value of the residual of the earnings prediction model (PRIV_INF)	Logistic transformation of the R^2 of the fitted stock comovement model (stock comovement)	Hagendorff et al. (2013)
Asymmetric information index (IN_ASYMMETRY)	Distance to default (DTD)	Vallascas and Keasey (2013)
Analyst forecast errors (AFE); analysts forecast dispersion (AFD)	Z-score, Z-score (CAR), Z-score (ROA) Systematic risk according to the market mode (SYSR) Idiosyncratic risk according to the market model (IDIO)	Fosu et al. (2017)
Timely recognition of expected loan losses (TR) in LLP Abnormal loan loss provisions (ALLPs)	Total, systematic, and idiosyncratic risk components (TOT, SYS, and IDIO)	Kim et al. (2020)
The ratio of available-for-sales securities The ratio of off-balance sheet items	Z-score The standard deviation of return on assets (σROA)	Cao and Juelsrud (2022)
Discretionary loan loss provisions (DLLPs)	Z-score	Tran et al. (2022)
OpacityFE: bank opacity measures in 12-month analysts' forecast error, abs((12-month-forecast EPS–actual EPS)/price) OpacityDis: forecast dispersion (σ 12-month-forecast EPS)	Delta conditional value at risk according to Adrian and Brunnermeier (ΔCoVaR) Marginal expected shortfall (MES)	Mies (2024)

prices. Investors negatively perceive the introduction of this regulation, with more pronounced reactions for poorly transparent, large, and complex banks located in countries with high exposure to sovereign indebtedness.

References

Acharya, V. V., & Ryan, S. G. (2016). Banks' financial reporting and financial system stability. *Journal of Accounting Research, 54*(2), 277–340.

Admati, A. R., & Pfleiderer, P. (2000). Forcing firms to talk: Financial disclosure regulation and externalities. *The Review of Financial Studies, 13*(3), 479–519.

Akhigbe, A., McNulty, J. E., & Stevenson, B. A. (2013). How does transparency affect bank financial performance? *International Review of Financial Analysis, 29*, 24–30.

Akhigbe, A., McNulty, J. E., & Stevenson, B. A. (2017). Additional evidence on transparency and bank financial performance. *Review of Financial Economics, 32*, 1–6.

Allen, F., & Carletti, E. (2008). Mark-to-market accounting and liquidity pricing. *Journal of Accounting and Economics, 45*(2–3), 358–378.

Allen, F., & Gale, D. (2000). Corporate governance and competition. *Corporate Governance: Theoretical and Empirical Perspectives, 23*(4), 23–94.

Allen, F., & Gale, D. (2004). Competition and financial stability. *Journal of Money, Credit and Banking*, 453–480.

Andries, K., Gallemore, J., & Jacob, M. (2017). The effect of corporate taxation on bank transparency: Evidence from loan loss provisions. *Journal of Accounting and Economics, 63*(2–3), 307–328.

Andrievskaya, I., & Semenova, M. (2016). Does banking system transparency enhance bank competition? Cross-country evidence. *Journal of Financial Stability, 23*, 33–50.

Bakk-Simon, K., Borgioli, S., Giron, C., Hempell, H. S., Maddaloni, A., Recine, F., & Rosati, S. (2012). Shadow banking in the euro area: An overview. *ECB occasional paper*, (2012133).

Barth, J. R., Caprio, G., & Levine, R. (2001b). *The regulation and supervision of banks around the world: A new database* (Vol. 2588). World Bank Publications.

Barth, J. R., Caprio, G., Jr., & Levine, R. (2001a). Banking systems around the globe: Do regulation and ownership affect performance and stability? In *Prudential supervision: What works and what doesn't* (pp. 31–96). University of Chicago Press.

Barth, J. R., Caprio Jr, G., & Levine, R. (2004). Guide to the 2003 World Bank Survey.

Barth, J. R., Lin, C., Lin, P., & Song, F. M. (2009). Corruption in bank lending to firms: Cross-country micro evidence on the beneficial role of competition and information sharing. *Journal of Financial Economics, 91*(3), 361–388.

Barth, M. E., & Schipper, K. (2008). Financial reporting transparency. *Journal of Accounting, Auditing & Finance, 23*(2), 173–190.

Bauman, U., & Nier, E. (2003). Market Discipline and Financial Stability. *Bank of England Financial Stability Review.*

Beatty, A., & Liao, S. (2011). Do delays in expected loss recognition affect banks' willingness to lend? *Journal of Accounting and Economics, 52*(1), 1–20.

Beck, T., Maksimovic, V., & DemirgÃ¼Ã§-Kunt, A. (2003). Bank competition, financing obstacles, and access to credit. *Financing Obstacles, and Access to Credit (March 2003).*

Berger, A. N., & Bouwman, C. H. (2013). How does capital affect bank performance during financial crises? *Journal of Financial Economics, 109*(1), 146–176.

Berger, A. N., Klapper, L. F., & Turk-Ariss, R. (2017). Bank competition and financial stability. In *Handbook of competition in banking and finance* (pp. 185–204). Edward Elgar Publishing.

Berger, A. N., Miller, N. H., Petersen, M. A., Rajan, R. G., & Stein, J. C. (2005). Does function follow organizational form? Evidence from the lending practices of large and small banks. *Journal of Financial Economics, 76*(2), 237–269.

Berger, A. N., & Udell, G. F. (2002). Small business credit availability and relationship lending: The importance of bank organisational structure. *The Economic Journal, 112*(477), F32–F53.

Bernanke, B. S. (1983). *Non-monetary effects of the financial crisis in the propagation of the Great Depression* (No. w1054). National Bureau of Economic Research.

Billett, M. T., Flannery, M. J., & Garfinkel, J. A. (1995). The effect of lender identity on a borrowing firm's equity return. *The Journal of Finance, 50*(2), 699–718.

Bischof, J., & Daske, H. (2013). Mandatory disclosure, voluntary disclosure, and stock market liquidity: Evidence from the EU bank stress tests. *Journal of Accounting Research, 51*(5), 997–1029.

Bischof, J., Daske, H., Elfers, F., & Hail, L. (2022). A tale of two supervisors: Compliance with risk disclosure regulation in the banking sector. *Contemporary Accounting Research, 39*(1), 498–536.

Bischof, J., Foos, D., & Riepe, J. (2023). Does greater transparency discipline the loan loss provisioning of privately held banks? *European Accounting Review*, 1–31.

Bischof, J., Laux, C., & Leuz, C. (2021). Accounting for financial stability: Bank disclosure and loss recognition in the financial crisis. *Journal of Financial Economics, 141*(3), 1188–1217.

Breuer, M. (2021). How does financial-reporting regulation affect industry-wide resource allocation? *Journal of Accounting Research, 59*(1), 59–110.

Breuer, M., Hombach, K., & MÃ¼ller, M. A. (2022). When you talk, I remain silent: Spillover effects of peers' mandatory disclosures on firms' voluntary disclosures. *The Accounting Review, 97*(4), 155–186.

Bushman, R. M. (2014). Thoughts on financial accounting and the banking industry. *Journal of Accounting and Economics, 58*(2–3), 384–395.

Bushman, R. M., Hendricks, B. E., & Williams, C. D. (2015). Bank competition: Measurement, decision-making and risk profiles. *University of Michigan, Ross School of Business Working Paper, 1243*.

Bushman, R. M., Piotroski, J. D., & Smith, A. J. (2004). What determines corporate transparency? *Journal of Accounting Research, 42*(2), 207–252.

Bushman, R. M., & Williams, C. D. (2012). Accounting discretion, loan loss provisioning, and discipline of banks' risk-taking. *Journal of Accounting and Economics, 54*(1), 1–18.

Bushman, R. M., & Williams, C. D. (2015). Delayed expected loss recognition and the risk profile of banks. *Journal of Accounting Research, 53*(3), 511–553.

Cao, J., & Juelsrud, R. E. (2022). Opacity and risk-taking: Evidence from Norway. *Journal of Banking & Finance, 134*, 106010.

Chen, Q., Goldstein, I., Huang, Z., & Vashishtha, R. (2022). Bank transparency and deposit flows. *Journal of Financial Economics, 146*(2), 475–501.

Chen, Y., & Hasan, I. (2006). The transparency of the banking system and the efficiency of information-based bank runs. *Journal of Financial Intermediation, 15*(3), 307–331.

Claessens, S., & Laeven, L. (2004). What drives bank competition? Some international evidence. *Journal of Money, Credit and Banking*, 563–583.

Cordella, T., & Yeyati, E. L. (2002). Financial opening, deposit insurance, and risk in a model of banking competition. *European Economic Review, 46*(3), 471–485.

Costello, A. M., Granja, J., & Weber, J. (2019). Do strict regulators increase the transparency of banks? *Journal of Accounting Research, 57*(3), 603–637.

Cull, R., Senbet, L. W., & Sorge, M. (2005). Deposit insurance and financial development. *Journal of Money, Credit and Banking*, 43–82.

Dal Maso, L., Kanagaretnam, K., Lobo, G. J., & Terzani, S. (2018). The influence of accounting enforcement on earnings quality of banks: Implications of bank regulation and the global financial crisis. *Journal of Accounting and Public Policy, 37*(5), 402–419.

Dang, T. V., Gorton, G., HolmstrÃ¶m, B., & Ordonez, G. (2017). Banks as secret keepers. *American Economic Review, 107*(4), 1005–1029.

Darrough, M. N. (1993). Disclosure policy and competition: Cournot vs. Bertrand. *Accounting Review*, 534–561.

Daske, H., Hail, L., Leuz, C., & Verdi, R. (2008). Mandatory IFRS reporting around the world: Early evidence on the economic consequences. *Journal of Accounting Research, 46*(5), 1085–1142.

Dechow, P., Ge, W., & Schrand, C. (2010). Understanding earnings quality: A review of the proxies, their determinants and their consequences. *Journal of Accounting and Economics, 50*(2–3), 344–401.

DemirgÃ¼Ã§-Kunt, A., & Detragiache, E. (2005). Cross-country empirical studies of systemic bank distress: A survey. *National Institute Economic Review, 192*, 68–83.

Dewally, M., & Shao, Y. (2013). Financial derivatives, opacity, and crash risk: Evidence from large US banks. *Journal of Financial Stability, 9*(4), 565–577.

DeYoung, R., & Roland, K. P. (2001). Product mix and earnings volatility at commercial banks: Evidence from a degree of total leverage model. *Journal of Financial Intermediation, 10*(1), 54–84.

Distinguin, I., Rous, P., & Tarazi, A. (2006). Market discipline and the use of stock market data to predict bank financial distress. *Journal of Financial Services Research, 30*(2), 151–176.

Dou, Y., Ryan, S. G., & Zou, Y. (2014). *The effects of credit competition on banks' loan loss provision timeliness*. Working paper, NYU.

Elbannan, M. A., & Elbannan, M. A. (2015). Economic consequences of bank disclosure in the financial statements before and during the financial crisis: Evidence from Egypt. *Journal of Accounting, Auditing & Finance, 30*(2), 181–217.

Ernstberger, J., Link, B., Stich, M., & Vogler, O. (2017). The real effects of mandatory quarterly reporting. *The Accounting Review, 92*(5), 33–60.

Fiechter, P., & Zhou, J. (2016). The impact of the Greek sovereign debt crisis on European banks' disclosure and its economic consequences. *The International Journal of Accounting, 51*(1), 85–117.

Fosu, S., Ntim, C. G., Coffie, W., & Murinde, V. (2017). Bank opacity and risk-taking: Evidence from analysts' forecasts. *Journal of Financial Stability, 33*, 81–95.

Gallemore, J. (2023). Bank financial reporting opacity and regulatory intervention. *Review of Accounting Studies, 28*(3), 1765–1810.

Gilbert, R. A. (1990). Market discipline of bank risk: Theory and evidence. *Federal Reserve Bank of St. Louis Review, 72*(1), 3–18.

Giner, B., Allini, A., & Zampella, A. (2020). The value relevance of risk disclosure: An analysis of the banking sector. *Accounting in Europe, 17*(2), 129–157.

Glosten, L. R., & Milgrom, P. R. (1985). Bid, ask and transaction prices in a specialist market with heterogeneously informed traders. *Journal of Financial Economics, 14*(1), 71–100.

Goetz, M. R. (2018). Competition and bank stability. *Journal of Financial Intermediation, 35*, 57–69.

Goldstein, I., & Sapra, H. (2014). Should banks' stress test results be disclosed? An analysis of the costs and benefits. *Foundations and TrendsÂ® in Finance, 8*(1), 1–54.

Granja, J. (2013). The relation between bank resolutions and information environment: Evidence from the auctions for failed banks. *Journal of Accounting Research, 51*(5), 1031–1070.

Hagendorff, J., Keasey, K., & Vallascas, F. (2013). Size, risk, and governance in European banking.

Healy, P. M., Hutton, A. P., & Palepu, K. G. (1999). Stock performance and intermediation changes surrounding sustained increases in disclosure. *Contemporary Accounting Research, 16*(3), 485–520.

Healy, P. M., & Palepu, K. G. (2001). Information asymmetry, corporate disclosure, and the capital markets: A review of the empirical disclosure literature. *Journal of Accounting and Economics, 31*(1–3), 405–440.

Heinle, M. S., & Smith, K. C. (2017). A theory of risk disclosure. *Review of Accounting Studies, 22*, 1459–1491.

Hellmann, T. F., Murdock, K. C., & Stiglitz, J. E. (2000). Liberalization, moral hazard in banking, and prudential regulation: Are capital requirements enough? *American Economic Review, 91*(1), 147–165.

Hirshleifer, J. (1971). Suppression of inventions. *Journal of Political Economy, 79*(2), 382–383.

HorvÃ¡th, R., & VaÅ¡ko, D. (2016). Central bank transparency and financial stability. *Journal of Financial Stability, 22*, 45–56.

Jiang, L., Levine, R., Lin, C., & Xie, W. (2022). Deposit supply and bank transparency. *Management Science, 68*(5), 3834–3855.

Jones, J. S., Lee, W. Y., & Yeager, T. J. (2013). Valuation and systemic risk consequences of bank opacity. *Journal of Banking & Finance, 37*(3), 693–706.
Jordan, J. S., Peek, J., & Rosengren, E. S. (2000). The market reaction to the disclosure of supervisory actions: Implications for bank transparency. *Journal of Financial Intermediation, 9*(3), 298–319.
Jungherr, J. (2018). Bank opacity and financial crises. *Journal of Banking & Finance, 97*, 157–176.
Kanagaretnam, K., Lim, C. Y., & Lobo, G. J. (2014). Effects of international institutional factors on earnings quality of banks. *Journal of Banking & Finance, 39*, 87–106.
Kanodia, C., Singh, R., & Spero, A. E. (2005). Imprecision in accounting measurement: Can it be value enhancing? *Journal of Accounting Research, 43*(3), 487–519.
Keeley, M. C. (1990). Deposit insurance, risk, and market power in banking. *The American Economic Review*, 1183–1200.
Kim, J., Kim, M., & Kim, Y. (2020). Bank transparency and the market's perception of bank risk. *Journal of Financial Services Research, 58*, 115–142.
Landier, A., & Thesmar, D. (2011). Regulating systemic risk through transparency: Trade-offs in making data public. In *Risk topography: Systemic risk and macro modeling* (pp. 31–44). University of Chicago Press.
Landsman, W. R. (2006). Fair value accounting for financial instruments: Some implications for bank regulation.
Lang, M., Lins, K. V., & Maffett, M. (2012). Transparency, liquidity, and valuation: International evidence on when transparency matters most. *Journal of Accounting Research, 50*(3), 729–774.
Leuz, C. (2003). IAS versus US GAAP: Information asymmetry–based evidence from Germany's new market. *Journal of Accounting Research, 41*(3), 445–472.
Leuz, C., & Verrecchia, R. E. (2000). The economic consequences of increased disclosure. *Journal of Accounting Research*, 91–124.
Leuz, C., & Wysocki, P. D. (2016). The economics of disclosure and financial reporting regulation: Evidence and suggestions for future research. *Journal of Accounting Research, 54*(2), 525–622.
Longo, S., Fabrizi, M., & Parbonetti, A. (2024). Market reaction to EU Crd IV regulation in the banking industry. *Research in International Business and Finance.*
Madhavan, A. (1995). Consolidation, fragmentation, and the disclosure of trading information. *The Review of Financial Studies, 8*(3), 579–603.
Manganaris, P., Beccalli, E., & Dimitropoulos, P. (2017). Bank transparency and the crisis. *The British Accounting Review, 49*(2), 121–137.
Marcus, A. J. (1984). Deregulation and bank financial policy. *Journal of Banking & Finance, 8*(4), 557–565.
Mies, M. (2024). Bank opacity, systemic risk and financial stability. *Journal of Financial Stability, 70*, 101211.
Moreno, D., & Takalo, T. (2016). Optimal bank transparency. *Journal of Money, Credit and Banking, 48*(1), 203–231.
Morgan, D. P. (2002). Rating banks: Risk and uncertainty in an opaque industry. *American Economic Review, 92*(4), 874–888.
Morris, S., & Shin, H. S. (2002). Social value of public information. *American Economic Review, 92*(5), 1521–1534.
Muller, K. A., III, Riedl, E. J., & Sellhorn, T. (2011). Mandatory fair value accounting and information asymmetry: Evidence from the European real estate industry. *Management Science, 57*(6), 1138–1153.
Nier, E. W. (2005). Bank stability and transparency. *Journal of Financial Stability, 1*(3), 342–354.
Novotny-Farkas, Z. (2016). The interaction of the IFRS 9 expected loss approach with supervisory rules and implications for financial stability. *Accounting in Europe, 13*(2), 197–227.
Parlatore, C. (2015). Transparency and bank runs. *Available at SSRN 1685543.*
Plantin, G., Sapra, H., & Shin, H. S. (2008). Marking-to-market: Panacea or Pandora's box? *Journal of Accounting Research, 46*(2), 435–460.

Poshakwale, S., & Courtis, J. K. (2005). Disclosure level and cost of equity capital: Evidence from the banking industry. *Managerial and Decision Economics, 26*(7), 431–444.

Ruckes, M. (2004). Bank competition and credit standards. *Review of Financial Studies, 17*(4), 1073–1102.

Semenova, M. (2012). Market discipline and banking system transparency: Do we need more information? *Journal of Banking Regulation, 13*(3), 241–248.

Stenfors, A. (2018). Bid-ask spread determination in the FX swap market: Competition, collusion or a convention? *Journal of International Financial Markets, Institutions and Money, 54*, 78–97.

Tadesse, S. (2006). The economic value of regulated disclosure: Evidence from the banking sector. *Journal of Accounting and Public Policy, 25*(1), 32–70.

Toh, M. Y., & Jia, D. (2021). Do foreign ownership and home-host country distance matter? Evidence on the impact of bank market power on liquidity creation in a selected Southeast Asian country. *Research in International Business and Finance, 56*, 101350.

Tran, D. V., Hassan, M. K., Alam, A. W., & Dau, N. (2022). Banks' financial soundness during the COVID-19 pandemic. *Journal of Economics and Finance, 46*(4), 713–735.

Vallascas, F., & Keasey, K. (2013). The volatility of European banking systems: A two-decade study. *Journal of Financial Services Research, 43*, 37–68.

Verrecchia, R. E. (2001). Essays on disclosure. *Journal of Accounting and Economics, 32*(1–3), 97–180.

Welker, M. (1995). Disclosure policy, information asymmetry, and liquidity in equity markets. *Contemporary Accounting Research, 11*(2), 801–827.

Chapter 3
Bank Risk Disclosure: Toward Mandatory Nonfinancial Information

3.1 Risk Disclosure and Financial Reporting Activities

The financial collapse of European banks, which led to either bankruptcy or significant market losses during the global financial crisis (2009–2012), confirms the dangers related to inappropriate risk disclosures. Inadequate risk disclosure is an important factor contributing to the financial crisis because banks did not report enough information about the risks they were exposed to (Avgouleas, 2009). Information risk has been emphasized by linking it to the reliability of accounting numbers reported under a fair-value approach. Some critics argue that fair-value accounting exacerbated the severity of the 2008 financial crisis. The main allegations are that fair-value accounting contributes to excessive leverage in boom periods and leads to excessive write-downs in busts (Laux & Leuz, 2010). The value of banks' assets and liabilities classified at Level 3 of the fair-value hierarchy is harder to understand than those classified at Level 1 or 2. Thus, the far less precise Level 3 measures include unobservable inputs computed using price models, discounted cash flow methodologies, or other information reflecting the reporting entity's assumptions and judgments (Magnan et al., 2015; Yao et al., 2018). These inputs are subject to management manipulation and involve more information risks to financial statement users. For instance, the International Accounting Standards Board (IASB) limits Level 3 inputs when Level 1 and 2 measurements are unavailable. Previous studies focus on investors' perception of fair-value estimates reported under the fair-value hierarchy. These studies conclude that estimates that are subject to greater measurement uncertainty are perceived as less value-relevant (Song et al., 2010; Goh et al., 2015) and that firms with greater exposure to more opaque financial assets exhibit higher information risk and higher cost of capital (Riedl & Serafeim, 2011). Further studies document an interplay between mandatory and voluntary disclosure when banks follow a fair-value measurement approach. Chung et al. (2017) document that firms with more Level 3 assets are more likely to provide

© The Author(s), under exclusive license to Springer Nature Switzerland AG 2025

S. Longo, *Disclosure in Banking*, SIDREA Series in Accounting and Business Administration, https://doi.org/10.1007/978-3-031-84196-5_3

voluntary disclosure to mitigate information risk captured in market betas. Prior research (Song et al., 2010) suggests that the information uncertainty associated with more opaque fair-value assets can come from two sources:

1) Information asymmetry, because Level 2 and 3 fair-value estimates rely on managers' estimates of market inputs unobservable to firm outsiders
2) Estimation error, because with sufficient resource allocation, even the managers may be more precise in making these very complex estimates

The theoretical literature concerning the effects of increased disclosure on information asymmetry yields conflicting predictions. Diamond and Verrecchia (1991) contend that increased levels of corporate disclosure can have welfare benefits even when no new information is generated. Disclosure that converts private information into public information will reduce the information advantage of informed investors over uninformed investors, thereby increasing the liquidity of the firm's securities. However, information asymmetry could increase if public disclosure incentivizes increased private information production (McNichols & Trueman, 1994; Demski & Feltham, 1994). Moreover, recognition can have different effects on information asymmetry than disclosure. Thus, the direction of the net effect of fair-value measurement on information asymmetry is unclear.

Muller et al. (2011) investigate whether the requirement that European real estate firms disclose the fair values of their investment property assets under International Accounting Standard (IAS) 40 affected information asymmetry. They find that mandatory adopters who did not previously disclose fair values experience a larger reduction in the bid-ask spread than early voluntary adopters. This finding supports the notion that releasing private information on fair values reduces information asymmetry. In contrast, Ball et al. (2012) provide evidence that US banks' use of fair value for trading securities is associated with greater information asymmetry. Still, they find no spread increase for banks that previously used fair value voluntarily. They also find similar results for nontrading securities for which banks exercised the fair-value option introduced in 2007. They attribute these results to recognition effects and the consequent association with the contracting roles of financial reporting rather than disclosure. The information environment of European banks is generally less rich than that of their US counterparts. Therefore, it is unclear whether the improved disclosure effect of greater accounting completeness on information asymmetry relative to the contracting effects will be the same for European banks. Considering the value implications of gains and losses due to the changes in own credit risk, the IASB's intention when introducing the fair-value option for liabilities was to reduce earnings volatility associated with measurement mismatches. Although empirical evidence shows that banks typically use this option to better reflect the economic hedging between selected financial assets and liabilities (Fiechter, 2011; Chang et al., 2021), concerns arise regarding the inclusion of own credit risk in the fair-value measurement of financial liabilities (Financial Executives International, 2004). Based on an experimental study using certified public accountants as participants, Gaynor et al. (2011) provide evidence that own credit risk disclosures mandated in Statement of Financial Accounting Standards

(SFAS) No. 159 are not sufficient to avoid misleading interpretations: the participants were unable to associate a gain (loss) arising from changes in the fair value of liabilities with an increase (decrease) in credit risk. Using archival data, Schneider and Tran (2015) examine the informational effects of fair-value options for liability adoption and of own credit risk recognition. A sample of European International Financial Reporting Standards (IFRS) banks provides evidence that credit risk recognizers have lower bid-ask spreads than nonrecognizers and nonadopters of fair value option liabilities. Value relevance studies on credit risk recognition also provide mixed results. Cedergren et al. (2015) find that own credit risk is not associated with stock returns. When considering the amount of unrecognized intangible assets, they find that their credit risk positively relates to equity returns when these omitted assets are low. Bens et al. (2016) document that after receiving Securities and Exchange Commission (SEC) comment letters on fair-value accounting, firms with higher Level 3 assets experience decreased bid-ask spreads and stock return volatility (lower information asymmetry). Fontes et al. (2018) find that assets at fair value are associated with noticeably lower information asymmetry. This reduction is more than twice as large when banks recognize their credit risk. In addition, the bid-ask spread is incrementally lower for banks that provide more detailed narrative disclosures on their credit risk.

3.2 Risk Disclosure and Financial Information: The State of the Art

In addition to stricter financial accounting requirements, which address criticisms of fair value accounting (Laux & Leuz, 2010) and loan loss provisioning under previous accounting standards (Barth & Landsman, 2010; Bushman & Williams, 2012), regulators have also focused significantly on improving risk disclosure practices. Risk disclosure positively affects the cost of capital (Fiechter & Zhou, 2016), market liquidity (Bischof & Daske, 2013), and bank valuation (Elbannan & Elbannan, 2015). Banking risk disclosure has become complex because of combined rules established by different regulators and supervisors (Bischof et al., 2022). For example, European banks face numerous supranational risk disclosure regulations following the International Accounting Standards (IFRS) and other banking rules provided by the Basel Committee or other entities (see Fig. 3.1).

Nowadays, regulators are still working on risk disclosure because of the recent bank failures (i.e., Silicon Valley Bank and Credit Suisse in March 2023), which have again raised concerns about the role of transparency, already instituted due to previous banking crises. The main concerns about how to gain a higher level of bank transparency include the treatment of credit losses under the current expected credit loss (ECL) model and the role of stress testing in maintaining bank safety implemented after the 2007–0208 crisis.

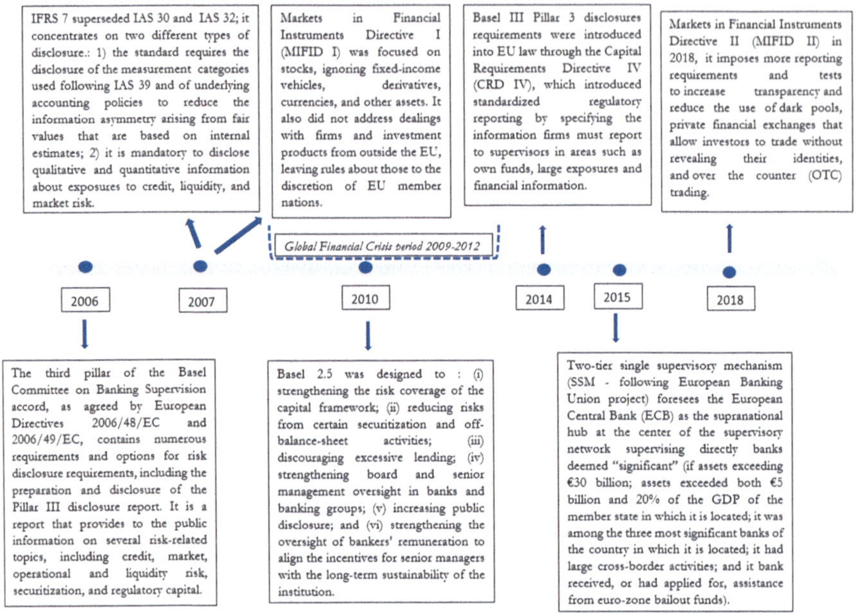

Fig. 3.1 Risk disclosure regulation in the EU banking industry from 2006

Financial reporting transparency has been emphasized, particularly in the new accounting regulation for loan loss provisioning under IFRS 9, which entered into force in 2018. This new standard foresees a real shift from an incurred loss approach to an expected current loss approach based on accounting for loan loss provisioning to measure impairment allowances. The approach for provisioning adopted before IFRS 9 was classified as "too little, too late" to absorb future potential loan losses. A bank's primary asset is its loan portfolio; therefore, understanding its performance and solvency depends on having accurate and timely information regarding loan losses. Delaying the extent to which loan portfolio deteriorations are incorporated into the provision creates uncertainty over the bank's loan portfolio's performance and bank fundamentals. Furthermore, when a bank delays the recognition of loan losses, financial indicators, such as earnings, will reflect deteriorations in bank fundamentals with a delay, and stakeholders' ability to interpret nonaccrual-based signals of bank health (such as the nonperforming loans ratio) will be negatively impacted. Delaying the recognition of expected loan losses (following IAS 39) also creates opacity by forcing reported capital to cover both expected and unexpected losses, leading to uncertainty regarding the bank's ability to absorb unexpected losses (Bushman & Williams, 2015). Table 3.1 highlights the key differences between IFRS 9, which took effect in 208, and its predecessor IAS 39. Based on IFRS 9, a new impairment model (three-stage model) has been established to classify financial instruments (loans) based on quality (rating of soundness), indicating

Table 3.1 Impairment model following IFRS9 and IAS 39

IFRS 9 from 2018	IAS 39 being replaced by IFRS 9
Stage 1 (Performing financial instrument): financial assets with high credit quality with a significant increase in credit risk since initial recognition or with low credit risk at the reporting date. Impairment provision is determined on a 12-month expected loss on the gross book value of the exposure. Stage 2 (Deteriorated financial instrument): financial assets with a significant increase in credit risk since the initial recognition. The impairment provision is determined based on lifetime expected loss. Stage 3 (Nonperforming financial instrument): financial assets with objective evidence of impairment at the reporting date. Impairment provision is determined based on the lifetime expected credit losses on the net book value of the exposure. Estimation of probability of default (PD): the estimation of PD considers different time horizons, depending on whether the instrument is classified in stage 1 (next 12 months) or stages 2–3 (remaining life).	Need for "objective evidence of impairment" with an observable loss event. "Trigger events" as indicators of objective evidence are provided by the standard (nonexclusive list).

the health of a bank's loan portfolio. Banks are required to periodically estimate expected credit losses and adjust loan loss provisions accordingly.

3.3 Risk Disclosure on the Interplay Between Accounting and Banking Regulations

At the time of the switch from IAS 39 to IFRS 9, banks were required to disclose the "day-one impact of IFRS 9," namely, the difference between provisions estimated under IFRS 9 and those same provisions under IAS 39. This disclosure offers a unique example of how disclosure could make a difference from a valuation perspective on the interplay between accounting and banking regulations. While general-purpose financial reporting provides information for the decision-making process, prudential bank regulation seeks to limit the frequency and cost of bank failures and protect the financial system by limiting the frequency and cost of systemic crises. On the one hand, these new disclosures based on IFRS 9 adoption drive higher predictive ability of ECL provisions when credit conditions deteriorate. On the other hand, the Basel Committee (bank regulator) assumes that provisions cover expected losses, whereas the required regulatory capital covers unexpected losses. Nevertheless, the loan loss provisioning of IFRS 9 is based on expected loss computations, which differ from the expected loss amount under the Basel regulation for several reasons:

1. The time horizon depends on which possible losses must be considered. The Basel framework is based on a 12-month horizon, whereas accounting standards consider the remaining lifetime of at least some or even all financial assets.

2. Economic conditions are treated differently. IFRS 9 obliges institutions to account for current economic conditions. In contrast, the Basel regulation considers loan loss provisions to be abstracted from macroeconomic risk.

Knowing how the two regulatory approaches to loan loss provisioning usually interact is necessary for a comprehensive understanding. Any provisioning directly lowers Common Equity Tier 1 (CET 1) on the liability side. However, the Basel Committee on Banking Supervision adjusts possible shortfalls in provisioning. If the Basel-expected loss exceeds the provisions, the difference must be deducted from the eligible CET 1. The exact number of provisions only affects the eligible regulatory capital if there is a shortfall. The excess directly lowers the eligible CET 1 if provisions exceed Basel-expected losses (the excess may be added up to 0.6% in risk-weighted assets (RWA) to Tier 2 capital). This case mainly occurs in recessions due to higher provision levels. As a result, the new accounting standards may require additional core Tier 1 capital during downturns. Policymakers argue that the incurred loss model underlying current loan loss accounting reinforces the procyclical effects of bank capital regulation and should, therefore, be changed to allow bank managers more discretion to incorporate forward-looking judgments into loan loss provisions. Bushman and Williams (2012) document that forward-looking provisioning designed to smoothen earnings dampens discipline over risk-taking, consistent with diminished transparency inhibiting outside monitoring. In contrast, forward-looking provisioning reflecting the timely recognition of expected future loan losses is associated with enhanced risk-taking discipline (Beatty & Liao, 2011). These considerations are particularly relevant in the context of further recent health crises. The wake of the COVID-19 outbreak in 2020 raised the concern that IFRS 9 could exacerbate the economic crisis. While usually inducing less procyclicality than the incurred credit loss (ICL) model, the ECL model could have a procyclical effect when the economic downturn is extremely sudden and severe, as seen in situations like the COVID-19 crisis. Such concern was plausible, especially observing that in situations of adverse credit conditions, the ECL model results in a significant increase in provisions. This could exacerbate a crisis to the extent that higher provisions reduce the volume of credit by decreasing bank profitability.

3.4 Stress Tests Disclosure: A Further Perspective on Risks

In the new era of financial regulation following the crisis of 2007–2008, central banks worldwide conduct periodic stress tests for financial institutions to assess their ability to withstand future shocks. An important aspect of this regulation is that the results of these stress tests are meant to be disclosed publicly. These stress test disclosures are prominent disclosures that link financial reporting and capital adequacy calculations, increasing the banking system's safety. There remains disagreement about the effects of disclosing the results of those stress tests to market participants. Goldstein and Sapra (2014) argue that stress tests provide information for the market and regulators to discipline bank risk-taking and ensure financial stability. Nevertheless, they acknowledge that banks aiming at passing stress tests could take inefficient actions rather than engage in prudent risk-taking. Goldstein and Yang's findings (2019) document that when disclosure provides information that real decision-makers care to learn about, disclosure negatively affects price informativeness and potentially negatively impacts real efficiency due to public disclosures crowding out other types of private information discovery. However, disclosure might be harmful because it reduces economic agents' future risk-sharing opportunities. If banks are exposed to random liquidity shocks, they will create arrangements among themselves or with outside markets to insure themselves against such shocks. Public information about the state of each bank and its ability to withstand future shocks could limit these hedging opportunities, thereby generating a welfare loss (Goldstein & Leitner, 2018). Recent empirical evidence supports the view that stress tests provided useful information to market participants during the recent crises (Peristiani et al., 2010; Bayazitova & Shivdasani, 2012; Ellahie, 2013; Greenlaw et al., 2012). Stress tests have become an important component of the supervisory toolkit, and their main characteristics can be identified as follows:

1. They are forward-looking.
2. They generally put much weight on highly adverse scenarios, providing supervisors with information about tail risks.
3. Common scenarios are applied to banks to apply consistent supervisory standards across banks.
4. Unlike traditional supervisory examinations that are generally kept confidential, the results of bank stress tests are frequently publicly disclosed to restore confidence and reduce market uncertainty.

However, the extent of disclosure of stress-test results remains controversial. Indeed, the introduction of the stress test was greeted with a mixture of trepidation and skepticism by financial analysts, with some worrying that undercapitalized banks would be closed or nationalized based on the test results and others expecting a "whitewash," in which even undercapitalized banks would be given a pass. Bischof and Daske (2013) note that the first stress test for the European banking industry was in 2010, involving 91 banks. The Committee of European Banking Supervisors (CEBS), the predecessor institution of the European Banking Authority (EBA), published firm-level information about the results of the stress test simulations. Simultaneously, CEBS and national regulators encouraged all participating banks to individually disclose detailed information on their aggregate exposure at default (EAD) to central and local government debt. Eighty-one participants met this request and released short statements detailing their sovereign exposure in the trading and banking books. Compared with other mandated disclosures, the supervisory credit risk disclosures that were part of the stress tests are unique in at least two ways. First, the level of mandatory detail of the disclosures significantly exceeded the minimum credit risk disclosures required by IFRS 7 and Pillar 3 of the Basel II Framework. Second, the standardization of tabular disclosure overcomes the heterogeneity frequently observed in the risk disclosure formats of international financial institutions. The content of the first stress tests (2011) was based on:

1. Data on risk-weighted assets and own funds: the latter included a breakdown of items recognized as core Tier 1 by EBA, compulsory deductions, governmental support, and other mitigating measures fully committed by 30 April 2011.
2. Key profit and loss (P&L) figures, including net interest income, trading income, impairments, other income/losses, and net profit after tax; details on provisions, loss rates, and coverage ratios for performing and nonperforming exposures, with separate evidence on retail, corporate, bank, and sovereign portfolios.
3. A breakdown of credit exposures by geographic area, counterparty, and default status.
4. A breakdown of sovereign exposures by geographic area, accounting treatment (e.g., trading book, fair value option, available for sale, etc.), and duration band: this included derivative exposures at fair value.

A further debated aspect is the contribution of stress test disclosure as additional information available for market participants. In frictionless markets, more information is always better for a decision-maker (Blackwell's theorem). However, more information does not necessarily imply an improvement when operating in an environment with asymmetric information. The proponents of public information disclosure argue that it disciplines markets, reduces adverse selection, and improves price informativeness. There are also arguments why public information disclosure can be harmful. Releasing information about the future state of the economy destroys ex ante risk-sharing incentives. Goldstein and Leitner (2018) find that disclosing too much destroys risk-sharing, but disclosing too little might result in a market breakdown during a crisis. Andolfatto et al. (2014) show that it is only optimal to disclose information to prevent agents from costly acquisition. Alvarez and Barlevy (2015) show in a model of the information spillover that the decision to disclose depends on the presence of contagion. Furthermore, Gigler et al. (2014) indicate that frequent disclosure requirements may lead to managers' short-termism. Prior contributions about stress test disclosure identify positive and negative effects (see Table 3.2). We see that most (but not all) studies conclude that stress tests produce (some) valuable information for market participants and can play a role in mitigating bank opacity (positive effects of stress test disclosure). The second strand of related literature examines to what extent supervisory information should be disclosed. Several of these studies conclude that it may only sometimes be optimal to fully disclose stress test results (negative effects of stress test disclosure).

Table 3.2 Literature background about stress test disclosure—positive and negative effects in capital markets

Positive effects of bank stress test disclosure	Author(s)-year
Although the market had correctly anticipated which banks would have a capital gap, the US Supervisory Capital Assessment Program (SCAP) was informative about the size of the gap.	Peristiani et al. (2010)
Information asymmetry declined for tested banks after disclosing Europe's 2011 stress test results.	Ellahie (2013)
Stress tests carry useful information to the market based on a standard event study approach.	Petrella and Resti (2013) and Bird et al. (2023)
Stress test disclosure increases voluntary disclosure once the test results are publicly announced, increasing the bid-ask spread (higher market liquidity signals higher transparency).	Bischof and Daske (2013)
Stock and CDS markets may react differently because stockholders and creditors may have different incentives to disclose stress test information.	Georgescu et al. (2017)
Stress tests result in safer banks regarding capital ratios and risk-weighted asset ratios.	Acharya et al. (2018)
Stress tests have helped counter the procyclicality of bank capital and improved risk management and capital planning at tested institutions. Tested banks increased loan spreads relative to nontested banks and reduced the availability of loans, most particularly riskier ones.	Kohn and Liang (2019)
Stress test announcements reduce bank systemic risk.	Sahin et al. (2020)
Stress tests do not increase information asymmetry or uncertainty; moreover, they do not incentivize the generation of private information.	Fernandes et al. (2020)

Negative effects of bank stress test disclosure	Author(s)-year
Stress tests uncover unique information to outsiders; there are also potential endogenous costs associated with such disclosure. For instance, disclosure might interfere with the operation of the interbank market and the risk sharing provided in this market.	Goldstein and Sapra (2014)
Under normal circumstances (different from crisis conditions), releasing stress test outcomes may not surprise markets. The outcomes of stress tests are, to a large extent, predictable.	Schuermann (2014); Ahnert et al. (2018)
Stress-tested banks do not significantly change their loan portfolio composition in response to stress-testing results nor reduce interbank borrowing and lending.	Flannery et al. (2017)
Stress-tested banks lower dividends significantly more than non-stress-tested banks.	Cornett et al. (2020)
Stress test disclosure lowers the expected risk-adjusted profits for a nonnegligible fraction of banks. The magnitude of this effect depends on the banking system's structure; alarmingly, it is more pronounced for systemically important institutions.	Goncharenko et al. (2018)
Stress test disclosures are associated with a reduction in analyst coverage and firm-specific information in forecasts.	Heitz and Wheeler (2023)

3.5 Risk Disclosure and Managerial Discretion

Regulators promote disclosure in banking, while bank managers desire good disclosure from their clients, particularly borrowers. Commercial banks live on private information they gather from their customers, particularly small and medium enterprises (e.g., Diamond, 1984; Ramakrishnan & Thakor, 1984). Following a loan issuing process, banks screen this information before loans are made by monitoring after loans are issued and, in some cases, by collecting data from prior relationships, including lending and other connections. Banks tend to keep loans they originate entirely on their balance sheets until maturity. The quality of a bank's loan portfolio depends on the information quality of its borrowers. By closely scrutinizing borrowers and obtaining more reliable information, banks can reduce their credit risk exposure, leading to lower loan loss provisions and a decreased likelihood of nonperforming loans (Gallimberti, 2021). Borrowers' transparency can affect a bank's credit practices and risk-taking behavior by improving the quality of loans. Ertan et al. (2017) employed a novel disclosure initiative introduced by the European Central Bank in 2013 to facilitate the securitization process. They found that securitized loans that originated under the transparency regime are of better quality, with a lower default probability, a lower delinquent amount, fewer days in delinquency, and lower losses upon default. Additionally, banks with more intensive loan-level information collection and those operating under stronger market discipline experience greater improvement in their loan quality under the new reporting standards. Transparent reporting initiatives in the banking sector reduce information asymmetry among lenders and enhance borrowers' credit access (Djankov et al., 2007; Liberti et al., 2022; Sutherland, 2020). It is necessary to explore the effect of transparency on the way banks internally process information in lending decisions (Ryan, 2017, 2018). Kang et al. (2021) investigate whether compliance with transparent reporting rules fosters the harmonization of a bank's credit standards across its geographic regions. They find that harmonization increases following the adoption of the new reporting rules, showing an increase in more favorable lending terms to borrowers and higher loan quality for banks. This incentivizes banks to improve their internal decision-making and thereby reduce regional divergence in their credit standards. In a further study, Balakrishnan and Ertan (2018) examine the effects of banks' financial reporting frequency from 2000 to 2014 and find that quarterly reporting improves their loan portfolio quality. After switching to quarterly financial disclosures, banks experience a relative decrease of about 11% in nonperforming loans. This last study by Balakrishnan and Ertan (2018) recalls the experience at the European country level when the EU Transparency Directive (TD) issued in 2004 required listed firms (including banks) in member countries to release qualitative or quantitative interim management statements (IMSs) of financial position and performance in the first and third quarters, usually including earnings information (Christensen et al., 2016; Ernstberger et al., 2017). Nevertheless, regulators issued an amendment directive that abolished the quarterly reporting requirement, effective November 2015, to promote a long-term corporate focus and reduce the burden of preparing frequently released financial reports (Nallareddy et al., 2021). This regulatory experience for bank transparency highlights critical aspects that could be hard to foresee. Greater reporting frequency can improve bank loan quality (disciplining effect) or induce excessive risk-taking (myopic effect). Frequently disseminated financial information allows market participants to be informed on time. In this way, managers do not fall into the temptation of engaging in excessive risk-taking. In keeping with this view, Kanodia and Lee (1998) and Gigler et al. (2014) show that the anticipation of periodic performance reports has a disciplining effect on managers' ex ante investment decisions, thus reducing overinvestment. Moreover, frequent reporting can also improve supervisory discipline, which could also affect banks' ex ante incentives (Stephanou, 2010). Regulators can use the price movements of bank securities as an intervention (Hovakimian & Kane, 2000; Kane, 2004; Flannery & Thakor, 2006). Further, increased reporting allows market participants to pressure bank regulators to intervene in troubled banks (Rochet, 2008). Due to greater financial reporting frequency, the increased disciplinary force exercised by market participants and regulators could result in banks extending better quality loans and not indulging in excessive risk-taking (disciplining effect).

In contrast to the above arguments, increasing the frequency of financial reporting could lead managers to make myopic decisions. Stein (1989) suggests that managers may be tempted to boost short-term stock prices at the expense of long-term profitability. Banks face pressure to maintain high stock prices from capital markets and regulators, which may use observed prices to intervene. Banks operate in environments where their actions are opaque, hard to verify, and susceptible to risk-shifting. In conclusion, banks may choose opportunistic portfolios to meet the expectations of capital markets or regulators, but these actions may reduce their long-term value. Taking more risks is a convenient way to increase short-run profitability in banking. Banks can relax lending standards, increasing their loan yield and impacting default rates (Balakrishnan & Ertan, 2018). This suggests that increasing reporting frequency may cause banks to lend to risky borrowers, resulting in short-term income but affecting long-term balance sheet strength (myopic effect). Another issue of greater reporting frequency for banks is that it could lead to inefficient bank runs driven by coordination failures among depositors and short-run creditors (Diamond & Dybvig, 1983). While depositors care about how well capitalized or solvent a bank is, they are also mindful of what other market participants believe about its financial condition. Thus, frequent reporting could impair market discipline (Holmstrom, 2015; Gorton, 2015). Balakrishnan and Ertan (2018) conclude that banks reduce nonperforming loans when they adopt quarterly reports. Still, this effect is stronger in regimes with weaker depositor insurance and external monitoring and those with stronger capital markets. They also find that banks that provide quarterly financial information experience lower deposit interest rates and credit default swap spreads. In other words, banks, by using frequent reports, increase transparency, reduce risk-taking, and are perceived as more stable and conservative. Given these factors, bankers are aware of their ability to signal their bank's stability and profitability through the quality of the loan portfolio. Their advantage lies in having superior information relative to investors and other stakeholders regarding default risks inherent in their loan portfolios.

3.6 Risk Disclosure and the Shift to Mandatory Nonfinancial Information: A New Dimension

For a long time, the banking industry was not under compulsion to include environmental, social, and governance (ESG) aspects nor to produce nonfinancial information. Unlike the rest of the corporate world, which was much more engaged in social responsibility, banks only started producing nonfinancial information about their role in the decarbonization transition when a series of events—i.e., natural disasters, the COVID-19 emergency, and the Sustainable Development Goals (SDGs) introduced by the UN 2030 Agenda—occurred, leading to an increase in social and environmental awareness (Cosma et al., 2020). Their direct involvement with borrowers engaged in aggressive industrialization to generate profits, while claiming environmental responsibility, became a significant concern. As a result, it emerged as a risk that needed to be addressed and disclosed. Banks are connected to environmental degradation through their financing of manufacturing firms that contribute to the pollution of land, air, and water through harmful production processes. We all agree that banks have a rather small direct impact on the environment because of their low levels of direct emissions and relatively limited use of resources compared to other industries (Weber et al., 2014). Nevertheless, banks play an important role in economic development since they decide how to allocate financial resources to different firms and sectors. At the same time, banks have the power to address more sustainable corporate behaviors. In this perspective, the Non-Financial Reporting Directive (Directive 2014/95/EU) guides how banks and insurance companies should look at the recommended nonfinancial disclosure from the point of view of their business activities, including lending, investing, insurance underwriting, and asset management activities (Del Gaudio et al., 2022; Bedendo et al., 2023).

In a study conducted by Cosma et al. (2020), we learned that from 2018, not all EU banks (mostly commercial banks) published their nonfinancial disclosure in English, as required by the Directive, and only 89 listed banks and other 173 nonlisted banks did it. Löw et al. (2019) explore the determinants of nonfinancial reports in 76 EU banks for 2017 and 2018, before and after the implementation of the EU Directive 2014, which imposed a transition from voluntary to mandatory nonfinancial disclosure. Each European country had to integrate the Directive into national laws by 2016. More specifically, the Directive allows member states to impose country-specific requirements on companies regarding the reporting framework, the disclosure format, and the reporting content. First, Italian banks obtained the highest score, both in 2017 and in 2018, in terms of the extent of disclosure, compared to other European banks. Second, the researchers noted that it was very difficult to understand the implementation of the EU Directive when analyzing only 2 years of data. In this direction, Schröder (2022) conducted a study to assess the nonfinancial reporting quality (NFRQ) in the mandatory NFR of the 100 largest banks operating in Germany over 3 years and identified reporting-level determinants (experience, format, framework, and audit) that impact NFRQ. His findings indicate that banks view their stakeholder engagement activities as stakeholder management or public relations strategies. Banks also reported relatively detailed information on combating bribery and corruption. NFR provides a detailed level of reporting on labour practices, likely because banks are in constant competition for talent. These responsibility-driven initiatives can enhance employee retention and satisfaction. Another reason could be the historically high and unionized employee involvement that companies in Germany have to contend with.

The EU Directive, by transitioning from voluntary to mandatory non-financial reporting, significantly influenced banking behaviour. Managers were forced to focus on identifying the tools and practices necessary to comply with this new regulation (Korca et al., 2021). A potential greenwashing issue also emerged in the banking sector, where banks might have exaggerated their ESG performance to distract from or conceal poor practices. Initially, the focus was on environmental concerns, but over time, banks began addressing social issues, particularly diversity, equality, and inclusion (DEI), which shifted their organizational priorities and the way they assessed their borrowers. The huge pressure from the three giants—Blackrock, Vanguard, and State Street—has completely changed the manner of disclosing nonfinancial information (Bonacchi et al., 2022). Additionally, the existence of a corporate social responsibility (CSR) committee in European banks has helped achieve a moderate level of compliance, particularly in terms of providing complete information. However, there is still a significant need for improvement in their forward-looking strategies. (Cosma et al., 2022; Gurol & Lagasio, 2022). Veltri's book (2020) deeply considers the value and relevance of nonfinancial risk. There, she highlights that nonfinancial risk is primarily based on a reputational risk that could damage a company's business. From a banking perspective, corporate nonfinancial risk could directly impact credit risk, worsening the quality of loan portfolios. Measuring nonfinancial risks becomes challenging since it is hard to distinguish between financial and nonfinancial risks. The EU Directive regulation has two key expectations. First, banks' ESG ratings should contribute to a reduction in non-performing loans (Liu et al., 2023). Second, banks are encouraged to adopt more sustainable financing practices, prioritizing support for eco-friendly economic development, which in turn improves their own ESG scores. On the other hand, the ESG ratings of their borrowers should be the main drivers during the lending process, ensuring higher accuracy in their credit valuation process and enhancing their loans' portfolio quality (Wang, 2023).

The quality (particularly materiality and reliability) of nonfinancial information is undoubtedly an important issue to investigate. Recent studies are addressing the reporting quality of nonfinancial bank reports in the wake of the Directive by examining their determinants. Gai et al. (2023) propose a methodology to apply a new tool, called BESGI (banks' environmental, social, governance, and indirect impacts), to assess banks' actual ESG disclosure by emphasizing the consistency of the results achieved and communicated by financial institutions. Veltri et al. (2023) conducted a case study on the biggest cooperative Italian bank and examined whether nonfinancial disclosure improved once the EU Directive took effect. They showed how this bank started to disclose specific aspects in nonfinancial areas every year, as required by the Italian decree, once it adopted the EU Directive into law at the country level. They detailed nonfinancial information for each environmental, social, and governance pillar, highlighting the big debate around "social" items like supporting local communities, businesses, and households; paying constant attention to customer needs; and improving moral, cultural, and economic conditions. These aspects are extremely important because they reflect the local communities' beliefs that impact the labor market. Banks are called to understand these phenomena since they support local economic growth. Nondiscrimination and human rights are other areas that are now inseparable from the assessments conducted on banks and their borrowers' companies. The expected changes should come from the bank's top management, particularly the board, which should address these policies from the top down. An existing example is through their board gender diversity (Gallego-Sosa et al., 2021). In the banking sector's commitment to the 2030 Agenda, a change is expected, thanks to the social actions carried out by companies and the dissemination of this information through reports. This provides a springboard for future research by offering a set of measures and analyses for interpreting heterogeneous economic scenarios.

References

Acharya, V. V., Berger, A. N., & Roman, R. A. (2018). Lending implications of US bank stress tests: Costs or benefits? *Journal of Financial Intermediation, 34*, 58–90.

Ahnert, L., Vogt, P., Vonhoff, V., & Weigert, F. (2018). The impact of regulatory stress testing on bank's equity and CDS performance. *University of St. Gallen, Swiss Institute of Banking and Finance Working Paper.*

Alvarez, F., & Barlevy, G. (2015). *Mandatory disclosure and financial contagion* (No. w21328). National Bureau of Economic Research.

Andolfatto, D., Berentsen, A., & Waller, C. (2014). Optimal disclosure policy and undue diligence. *Journal of Economic Theory, 149*, 128–152.

Avgouleas, E. (2009). The global financial crisis, behavioural finance and financial regulation: In search of a new orthodoxy. *Journal of Corporate Law Studies, 9*(1), 23–59.

Balakrishnan, K., & Ertan, A. (2018). Banks' financial reporting frequency and asset quality. *The Accounting Review, 93*(3), 1–24.

Ball, R., Jayaraman, S., & Shivakumar, L. (2012). Mark-to-market accounting and information asymmetry in banks. *Chicago Booth Research Paper*, (12-35).

Barth, M. E., & Landsman, W. R. (2010). How did financial reporting contribute to the financial crisis? *European Accounting Review, 19*(3), 399–423.

Bayazitova, D., & Shivdasani, A. (2012). Assessing tarp. *The Review of Financial Studies, 25*(2), 377–407.

Beatty, A., & Liao, S. (2011). Do delays in expected loss recognition affect banks' willingness to lend? *Journal of Accounting and Economics, 52*(1), 1–20.

Bedendo, M., Nocera, G., & Siming, L. (2023). Greening the financial sector: Evidence from bank green bonds. *Journal of Business Ethics, 188*(2), 259–279.

Bens, D. A., Cheng, M., & Neamtiu, M. (2016). The impact of SEC disclosure monitoring on the uncertainty of fair value estimates. *The Accounting Review, 91*(2), 349–375.

Bird, A., Karolyi, S. A., & Ruchti, T. (2023). Supervisory sentiment: Evidence from stress test disclosures. *Available at SSRN 2626058.*

Bischof, J., & Daske, H. (2013). Mandatory disclosure, voluntary disclosure, and stock market liquidity: Evidence from the EU bank stress tests. *Journal of Accounting Research, 51*(5), 997–1029.

Bischof, J., Daske, H., Elfers, F., & Hail, L. (2022). A tale of two supervisors: Compliance with risk disclosure regulation in the banking sector. *Contemporary Accounting Research, 39*(1), 498–536.

Bonacchi, M., Klein, A., Longo, S., & Strampelli, G. (2022). The effects of credible voluntary disclosures: Institutional investor engagement and investees' ESG performances. *European Corporate Governance Institute-Law Working Paper, 2022 (620).*

Bushman, R. M., & Williams, C. D. (2012). Accounting discretion, loan loss provisioning, and discipline of banks' risk-taking. *Journal of Accounting and Economics, 54*(1), 1–18.

Bushman, R. M., & Williams, C. D. (2015). Delayed expected loss recognition and the risk profile of banks. *Journal of Accounting Research, 53*(3), 511–553.

Cedergren, M. C., Chen, C., & Chen, K. (2015). *The implication of unrecognized intangible assets on the relation between market valuation and debt valuation adjustment.* Working Paper, SSRN.

Chang, Y. L., Liu, C. C., & Ryan, S. G. (2021). Accounting policy choice during the financial crisis: Evidence from adoption of the fair value option. *Journal of Accounting, Auditing & Finance, 36*(1), 108–141.

Christensen, H. B., Hail, L., & Leuz, C. (2016). Capital-market effects of securities regulation: Prior conditions, implementation, and enforcement. *The Review of Financial Studies, 29*(11), 2885–2924.

Chung, S. G., Goh, B. W., Ng, J., & Yong, K. O. (2017). Voluntary fair value disclosures beyond SFAS 157's three-level estimates. *Review of Accounting Studies, 22*, 430–468.

Cornett, M. M., Minnick, K., Schorno, P. J., & Tehranian, H. (2020). An examination of bank behavior around Federal Reserve stress tests. *Journal of Financial Intermediation, 41*, 100789.

Cosma, S., Principale, S., & Venturelli, A. (2022). Sustainable governance and climate-change disclosure in European banking: The role of the corporate social responsibility committee. *Corporate Governance: The International Journal of Business in Society, 22*(6), 1345–1369.

Cosma, S., Venturelli, A., Schwizer, P., & Boscia, V. (2020). Sustainable development and European banks: A non-financial disclosure analysis. *Sustainability, 12*(15), 6146.

Del Gaudio, B. L., Previtali, D., Sampagnaro, G., Verdoliva, V., & Vigne, S. (2022). Syndicated green lending and lead bank performance. *Journal of International Financial Management & Accounting, 33*(3), 412–427.

Demski, J. S., & Feltham, G. A. (1994). Market response to financial reports. *Journal of Accounting and Economics, 17*(1–2), 3–40.

Diamond, D. W. (1984). Financial intermediation and delegated monitoring. *The Review of Economic Studies, 51*(3), 393–414.

Diamond, D. W., & Dybvig, P. H. (1983). Bank runs, deposit insurance, and liquidity. *Journal of Political Economy, 91*(3), 401–419.

Diamond, D. W., & Verrecchia, R. E. (1991). Disclosure, liquidity, and the cost of capital. *The Journal of Finance, 46*(4), 1325–1359.

Djankov, S., McLiesh, C., & Shleifer, A. (2007). Private credit in 129 countries. *Journal of Financial Economics, 84*(2), 299–329.

Elbannan, M. A., & Elbannan, M. A. (2015). Economic consequences of bank disclosure in the financial statements before and during the financial crisis: Evidence from Egypt. *Journal of Accounting, Auditing & Finance, 30*(2), 181–217.

Ellahie, A. (2013). Capital market consequences of EU bank stress tests. *Available at SSRN 2157715.*
Ernstberger, J., Link, B., Stich, M., & Vogler, O. (2017). The real effects of mandatory quarterly reporting. *The Accounting Review, 92*(5), 33–60.
Ertan, A., Loumioti, M., & Wittenberg-Moerman, R. (2017). Enhancing loan quality through transparency: Evidence from the European Central Bank loan level reporting initiative. *Journal of Accounting Research, 55*(4), 877–918.
Fernandes, M., Igan, D., & Pinheiro, M. (2020). March madness in Wall Street: (What) does the market learn from stress tests? *Journal of Banking & Finance, 112*, 105250.
Fiechter, P. (2011). The effects of the fair value option under IAS 39 on the volatility of bank earnings. *Journal of International Accounting Research, 10*(1), 85–108.
Fiechter, P., & Zhou, J. (2016). The impact of the Greek sovereign debt crisis on European banks' disclosure and its economic consequences. *The International Journal of Accounting, 51*(1), 85–117.
Flannery, M., Hirtle, B., & Kovner, A. (2017). Evaluating the information in the federal reserve stress tests. *Journal of Financial Intermediation, 29*, 1–18.
Flannery, M., & Thakor, A. V. (2006). Accounting, transparency and bank stability. *Journal of Financial Intermediation, 15*(3), 281–284.
Fontes, J. C., Panaretou, A., & Peasnell, K. V. (2018). The impact of fair value measurement for bank assets on information asymmetry and the moderating effect of own credit risk gains and losses. *The Accounting Review, 93*(6), 127–147.
Gai, L., Bellucci, M., Biggeri, M., Ferrone, L., & Ielasi, F. (2023). Manuscript full title: Banks' ESG disclosure: A new scoring model. *Finance Research Letters, 57*, 104199.
Gallego-Sosa, C., Gutiérrez-Fernández, M., Fernández-Torres, Y., & Nevado-Gil, M. T. (2021). Corporate social responsibility in the European banking sector: Commitment to the 2030 agenda and its relationship with gender diversity. *Sustainability, 13*(4), 1731.
Gallimberti, C. M. (2021). Borrowers' financial reporting and the quality of banks' loan portfolios. *The Accounting Review, 96*(2), 261–301.
Gaynor, L. M., McDaniel, L., & Yohn, T. L. (2011). Fair value accounting for liabilities: The role of disclosures in unraveling the counterintuitive income statement effect from credit risk changes. *Accounting, Organizations and Society, 36*(3), 125–134.
Georgescu, O. M., Gross, M., Kapp, D., & Kok, C. (2017). Do stress tests matter? Evidence from the 2014 and 2016 stress tests.
Gigler, F., Kanodia, C., Sapra, H., & Venugopalan, R. (2014). How frequent financial reporting can cause managerial short-termism: An analysis of the costs and benefits of increasing reporting frequency. *Journal of Accounting Research, 52*(2), 357–387.
Goh, B. W., Li, D., Ng, J., & Yong, K. O. (2015). Market pricing of banks' fair value assets reported under SFAS 157 since the 2008 financial crisis. *Journal of Accounting and Public Policy, 34*(2), 129–145.
Goldstein, I., & Leitner, Y. (2018). Stress tests and information disclosure. *Journal of Economic Theory, 177*, 34–69.
Goldstein, I., & Sapra, H. (2014). Should banks' stress test results be disclosed? An analysis of the costs and benefits. *Foundations and Trends® in Finance, 8*(1), 1–54.
Goldstein, I., & Yang, L. (2019). Good disclosure, bad disclosure. *Journal of Financial Economics, 131*(1), 118–138.
Goncharenko, R., Hledik, J., & Pinto, R. (2018). The Negative effects of information disclosure: The dark side of the stress test. *Journal of Financial Stability, 37*, 49–59.
Gorton, G. B. (2015). *The maze of banking: History, theory, crisis*. Oxford University Press.
Greenlaw, D., Kashyap, A. K., Schoenholtz, K. L., & Shin, H. S. (2012). Stressed out: Macroprudential principles for stress testing. *Chicago Booth Research Paper*, (12-08).
Gurol, B., & Lagasio, V. (2022). Women board members' impact on ESG disclosure with environment and social dimensions: Evidence from the European banking sector. *Social Responsibility Journal, 19*(1), 211–228.

Heitz, A., & Wheeler, B. (2023). Bank stress test disclosures, private information production, and price informativeness. *Private Information Production, and Price Informativeness (June 7, 2023).*

Holmstrom, B. (2015). Understanding the role of debt in the financial system.

Hovakimian, A., & Kane, E. J. (2000). Effectiveness of capital regulation at US commercial banks, 1985 to 1994. *The Journal of Finance, 55*(1), 451–468.

Kane, E. J. (2004). Continuing dangers of disinformation in corporate accounting reports. *Review of Financial Economics, 13*(1–2), 149–164.

Kang, Y., Li, O. Z., & Lin, Y. (2021). Tax incidence in loan pricing. *Journal of Accounting and Economics, 72*(1), 101418.

Kanodia, C., & Lee, D. (1998). Investment and disclosure: The disciplinary role of periodic performance reports. *Journal of Accounting Research, 36*(1), 33–55.

Kohn, D., & Liang, N. (2019, July). Understanding the effects of the US stress tests. In *Federal Reserve System Conference: Stress testing: A discussion and review.*

Korca, B., Costa, E., & Farneti, F. (2021). From voluntary to mandatory non-financial disclosure following Directive 2014/95/EU: An Italian case study. *Accounting in Europe, 18*(3), 353–377.

Laux, C., & Leuz, C. (2010). Did fair-value accounting contribute to the financial crisis? *Journal of Economic Perspectives, 24*(1), 93–118.

Liberti, J., Sturgess, J., & Sutherland, A. (2022). How voluntary information sharing systems form: Evidence from a US commercial credit bureau. *Journal of Financial Economics, 145*(3), 827–849.

Liu, S., Jin, J., & Nainar, K. (2023). Does ESG performance reduce banks' nonperforming loans? *Finance Research Letters, 55*, 103859.

Löw, E., Klein, D., & Pavicevac, A. (2019). Corporate Social Responsibility Reports of European Banks–An Empirical Analysis of the Disclosure Quality and its Determinants.

Magnan, M., Menini, A., & Parbonetti, A. (2015). Fair value accounting: Information or confusion for financial markets? *Review of Accounting Studies, 20*, 559–591.

McNichols, M., & Trueman, B. (1994). Public disclosure, private information collection, and short-term trading. *Journal of Accounting and Economics, 17*(1–2), 69–94.

Muller, K. A., III, Riedl, E. J., & Sellhorn, T. (2011). Mandatory fair value accounting and information asymmetry: Evidence from the European real estate industry. *Management Science, 57*(6), 1138–1153.

Nallareddy, S., Pozen, R., & Rajgopal, S. (2021). Consequences of more frequent reporting: The UK experience. *Journal of Law, Finance, and Accounting, 6*(1), 51–88.

Peristiani, S., Morgan, D. P., & Savino, V. (2010). The information value of the stress test and bank opacity. *FRB of New York Staff Report*, (460).

Petrella, G., & Resti, A. (2013). Supervisors as information producers: Do stress tests reduce bank opaqueness? *Journal of Banking & Finance, 37*(12), 5406–5420.

Ramakrishnan, R. T., & Thakor, A. V. (1984). The valuation of assets under moral hazard. *The Journal of Finance, 39*(1), 229–238.

Riedl, E. J., & Serafeim, G. (2011). Information risk and fair values: An examination of equity betas. *Journal of Accounting Research, 49*(4), 1083–1122.

Rochet, J. C. (2008). Why are there so many banking crises. *The Politics and Policy of Bank Regulation, 33.*

Ryan, S. G. (2017). Do the effects of accounting requirements on banks' regulatory capital adequacy undermine financial stability? *Annual Review of Financial Economics, 9*, 1–20.

Ryan, S. G. (2018). Recent research on banks' financial reporting and financial stability. *Annual Review of Financial Economics, 10*, 101–123.

Sahin, C., de Haan, J., & Neretina, E. (2020). Banking stress test effects on returns and risks. *Journal of Banking & Finance, 117*, 105843.

Schneider, F., & Tran, D. H. (2015). On the relation between the fair value option and bid-ask spreads: Descriptive evidence on the recognition of credit risk changes under IFRS. *Journal of Business Economics, 85*, 1049–1081.

Schröder, P. (2022). Mandatory non-financial reporting in the banking industry: Assessing reporting quality and determinants. *Cogent Business & Management, 9*(1), 2073628.
Schuermann, T. (2014). Stress testing banks. *International Journal of Forecasting, 30*(3), 717–728.
Song, C. J., Thomas, W. B., & Yi, H. (2010). Value relevance of FAS No. 157 fair value hierarchy information and the impact of corporate governance mechanisms. *The Accounting Review, 85*(4), 1375–1410.
Stein, J. C. (1989). Efficient capital markets, inefficient firms: A model of myopic corporate behavior. *The Quarterly Journal of Economics, 104*(4), 655–669.
Stephanou, C. (2010). Rethinking market discipline in banking: Lessons from the financial crisis. *World Bank Policy Research Working Paper*, (5227).
Sutherland, A. G. (2020). Technology is changing lending: Implications for research. *Journal of Accounting and Economics, 70*(2–3), 101361.
Veltri, S. (2020). *Mandatory non-financial risk-related disclosure*. Springer International Publishing.
Veltri, S., Cristiano, E., & Ferraro, O. (2023). Examining the quality of the consolidated mandatory non-financial statements of a cooperative banking group: A longitudinal analysis. *Corporate Social Responsibility and Environmental Management, 30*(4), 1573–1587.
Wang, L. L. (2023). Transmission effects of ESG disclosure regulations through bank lending networks. *Journal of Accounting Research, 61*(3), 935–978.
Weber, O., Diaz, M., & Schwegler, R. (2014). Corporate social responsibility of the financial sector–strengths, weaknesses and the impact on sustainable development. *Sustainable Development, 22*(5), 321–335.
Yao, D., Percy, M., Stewart, J., & Hu, F. (2018). Determinants of discretionary fair value measurements: The case of Level 3 assets in the banking sector. *Accounting & Finance, 58*(2), 561–597.

Chapter 4
Climate Change Risk: The New Frontier in Banking Disclosure

4.1 Bringing the Environment into Bank Disclosure

Previous studies have argued that many benefits could be realized by increasing the level of information disclosed since managers in the banking sector could more easily oversee the environmental impact of their portfolios (Bolton & Kacperczyk, 2021). However, not only the quantity of information disclosed but also its quality could be relevant to stakeholders (Hooks & van Staden, 2011). The banking sector has received little attention from sustainable finance scholars regarding nonfinancial disclosure (Schröder, 2022), and previous studies have found that many banks are not disclosing enough information related to their environmental impact (Bolton & Kacperczyk, 2021). Despite the shift from voluntary to mandatory nonfinancial disclosure introduced by Directive 2014/95/EU, Schröder (2022) found that the nonfinancial disclosure of German banks is below average and is driven by experience, format, and framework. However, this shift has shaped overall banking risk disclosure and banks' behavior (Loew et al., 2019; Korca et al., 2021; Veltri et al., 2023). Environmental issues have particularly attracted bankers' attention, mostly because of the increase in natural disasters, which is tremendously affecting their borrowers (Dal Maso et al., 2022). Thus, environmental risks are on the agenda of regulatory processes, engaging particularly the banking industry as the main supporter of the economic development of a country.

In 1992, the international banking industry recognized the importance of lender environmental risk in the United Nations Environmental Program's "Statement by Banks on the Environment and Sustainable Development." Thompson and Cowton (2004) highlight that firms facing environmental risk must go through stringent lender monitoring before being approved when applying for a loan. Berthelot et al. (2003) document widespread evidence that the stock market reacts to new information on corporate exposure to environmental risk released by the news media and government regulators. Large (widely owned) firms that are members of environmentally sensitive industries are more likely to voluntarily disclose environmental

© The Author(s), under exclusive license to Springer Nature Switzerland AG 2025

S. Longo, *Disclosure in Banking*, SIDREA Series in Accounting and Business Administration, https://doi.org/10.1007/978-3-031-84196-5_4

information, especially when they are in the media spotlight due to involvement in an environmental accident, lawsuits, fines, attention from environmental lobby groups, or a high political profile. Environmental disclosure involves releasing information about firms' energy policies and pollution levels (i.e., carbon emission disclosure; GRI, 2013; Schiemann & Sakhel, 2019). Environmental disclosure is mainly concerned with reporting the impacts of corporate activities borne by others and with no direct financial consequences (i.e., corporate externalities). Because of the difficulties in getting a comprehensive overview of corporate environmental exposure, market participants must support high processing costs to assess this type of information.

But what is the role of environmental disclosure for banks? Do banks differ in how they address and assess environmental information?

- Firstly, banking environmental disclosure reveals banks' initiatives to reduce their climate footprint (e.g., decrease greenhouse gas emissions). Banks have increasingly emphasized their stewardship for achieving sustainability and climate goals, following a trend toward increasing their voluntary disclosure of environmental activities and footprints (e.g., Grewal & Serafeim, 2020; Christensen et al., 2021). Banks' environmental disclosures in reports used to communicate sustainability actions (e.g., sustainability reports, annual reports) are positively associated with:

  (i) A country's environmental risk and social attention toward sustainability topics (e.g., Ioannou & Serafeim, 2012, 2017; Baldini et al., 2018)
  (ii) A bank's reputation, environmental score ratings, and disclosure ratings (e.g., Serafeim, 2020; Basu et al., 2022; Christensen et al., 2022)
  (iii) A bank's green bond underwriting (e.g., Flammer, 2021; Lu, 2021; Baker et al., 2022; Bedendo et al., 2023)
  (iv) Customers' loyalty and lower cost of capital (e.g., Dhaliwal et al., 2011; Albuquerque et al., 2019)

- Secondly, banks are the first users of corporate environmental risk information in their lending activities (Aintablian et al., 2007), and today, they are particularly involved in the transition to a carbon-neutral economy. Corporate-effective environmental disclosure is a significant way for banks to collect more information about their borrowers and help them make better decisions to mitigate credit losses.

Banks have been perceived to be more responsible to their customers and to make more sustainable lending decisions (Hasan et al., 2022; Houston & Shan, 2022). Whether borrowers with additional environmental information or a higher degree of eco-friendliness can receive more financial support from banks has only recently been considered. Using a sample of listed Chinese manufacturing enterprises from 2012 to 2017, Xing et al. (2021) find that firms with higher environmental disclosure quality do not obtain more bank loans, but only when they are green and innovative do they usually access corporate loans. Giannetti et al. (2023) first analyzed the credibility of banks' environmental disclosures, indicating that features of banks' business models limit the relevance of their disclosures and the role that banks can play in guiding the transition to a green economy. Contrary to regulators' expectations, they find that banks reporting their activities as more sustainable are more prone to issue credit to borrowers in brown industries and to borrowers with higher emissions in general.

Banks commonly discuss their climate footprint in relation to their "finance" activities and "loan" decisions to portray their active contribution to a sustainable economy. Furthermore, banks' investor reports commonly discuss firms' environmental activities. They occasionally discuss the environment in connection with climate "risk." More visible and reputable banks disclose more environmental related information (e.g., Serafeim, 2020). Environmental disclosure pertains to the volume of firms' sustainability disclosures and environmental, social, and governance (ESG) ratings (e.g., Basu et al., 2022; Christensen et al., 2022). These disclosures should be positively related to environmental scores provided by reputable rating agencies, such as Morgan Stanley Capital International (MSCI) (MSCI Env score) and Sustainalytics (Sustainalytics Env score). Wang et al. (2023) built a proxy (independently from any ESG ratings) for environmental disclosures by collecting the investor reports of sample banks for the 2014–2020 period by developing a dictionary to capture environmental reporting choices within the banking context. Investor reports commonly discuss firms' environmental activities, including sustainability, nonfinancial information, and integrated reports. For instance, bank loans that are based on greenhouse gas (GHG) emissions data can be found in the Eurostat database. On the other hand, corporate-level GHG emission data can be retrieved from different data providers, such as Trucost, Institutional Shareholder Services (ISS), MSCI Carbon Disclosure Project (CDP), Sustainalytics, Thomson Reuters, Bloomberg, Urgentem, and RobecoSAM. Specifically, Trucost collects carbon emission data from publicly available sources, such as corporate websites, annual reports, corporate social responsibility (CSR) reports, the CDP (Carbon Disclosure Project), and direct communications with companies. The CDP is the world's largest (voluntary) climate risk disclosure platform. It is a global nonprofit organization founded in 2000 to help companies and cities disclose their environmental impact. The CDP began sending out requests for climate-related information in 2003 on behalf of 35 investors. As mentioned, the disclosure is voluntary, meaning it is not mandated by law or regulatory codes, such as annual reports and proxy statements, and may go beyond the basic requirements (e.g., UN Global Compact, Global Reporting Initiative—see later paragraph dedicated to the initiatives leading to guidelines and rules) (Fig. 4.1).

The data related to the GHG Protocol breaks down the total GHG emissions into three "scopes" (or levels):

- Scope 1 emissions relate to direct GHG emissions (i.e., sources that are owned or controlled by a company).
- Scope 2 emissions relate to emissions from purchased heat and electricity.
- Scope 3 emissions relate to emissions from the supply chain and other sources not owned or controlled by the company (e.g., employee business travel, outsourced business activities).

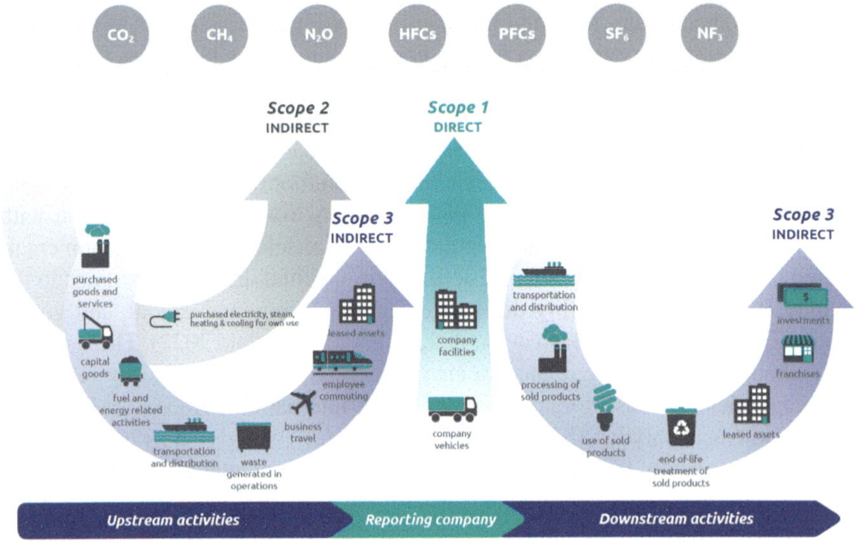

Fig. 4.1 Graphical representation of the Greenhouse Gas Protocol. *Scope 1* relates to direct emissions from the company as a result of the burning of fossil fuels during business operations. *Scope 2* emissions stem from electricity purchased from utility providers. The emissions can be higher or lower, depending on how this electricity is generated. *Scope 3* emissions are all the other indirect emissions from the value chain. This is further divided into upstream and downstream emissions. Upstream includes all indirect emissions from creating products and services, such as the capital goods a company uses and employee commuting, while downstream includes all indirect emissions from using products/services, such as the distribution and transportation of end products, and emissions associated with company investments. Scope 3 is divided into 15 categories that a company must report on. Finally, we note that in accordance with the Greenhouse Gas Protocol, all emissions are measured in tons of CO2 equivalents (tCO2e). Other greenhouse gases, like methane and dinitrogen oxide, have different potencies. Converting all greenhouse gases to CO2 potency can be compared and added to one final measure.

Here, I summarize the differences between the principal data providers of GHG emissions employed in the recent literature using disclosures and estimates from multiple channels (e.g., sustainability reports, news services, regulatory filings, and estimates from proprietary models—see Table 4.1).

Busch et al. (2022) show little variation in the reported scope 1 and 2 emission data across the data providers. Correlations in the reported scope 1 (scope 2) data average 0.99 (0.98) across the five providers: CDP, Trucost, MSCI, Sustainalytics, and Thomson Reuters. We must be cautious since there are differences across providers (see characteristics in Table 4.1 above) and data composition (particularly regarding scope 3 categories). For instance, for scope 3, there are also some profound differences between data providers. ISS is the only company reporting scope 3 on a total/aggregated level. Trucost provides scope 3 data on with a greater level of detail, specifically distinguishing between "upstream" and "downstream" activities. Upstream refers to the emissions generated during the production and transportation

Table 4.1 Summary of the main data providers on GHG emission data

GHG emission data provider	Description	Literature
Trucost	Data type: CO2e Scopes 1–3 Time period (years of emissions): from 2005 Total coverage: 14,000 companies Trucost collects carbon emission data from publicly available sources (corporate websites, annual reports, CSR reports, the CDP (Carbon Disclosure Project), and direct company communications). When a covered firm does not publicly disclose its carbon emissions, Trucost estimates a firm's annual carbon emissions based on an environmental profiling model. The model consists of four steps: (1) Analysis of company data: financial information is assessed to establish the primary business activities of an organization. Revenues from those activities are apportioned accordingly. (2) Mapping of company data: using the information in step 1, the environmental profiling model calculates an organization's direct and supply chain environmental impacts. (3) Incorporation of disclosures and public data: the analysis incorporates reported environmental data from public sources (such as annual reports and websites). Where environmental reporting is unavailable, Trucost draws on sources of proxy information (namely, fuel use or expenditure data), which can be converted into emission data. Reported figures are standardized for consistency. (4) Company verification process: each analyzed company is invited to verify or refine the environmental assessment conducted by Trucost.	Cohen et al. (2023), Azar et al. (2021), Bolton and Kacperczyk (2021), Aswani et al. (2024), Bonacchi et al. (2022)
ISS	Data type: CO2e Scopes 1–3 Time period (years of emissions): from 2005 Total coverage: 25,000 companies Includes company-reported data, third-party data, and estimations. Additional forward-looking climate risk data was provided.	Nguyen et al. (2023)
MSCI	Data type: CO2e Scopes 1–3 Time period (years of emissions): from 2008 Total coverage: 8500 companies Includes company-reported data, third-party data, and own estimations. MSCI Carbon Metrics provides additional information.	Swinkels and Markwat (2024), Azar et al. (2021), Gurvich and Creamer (2021)
Thomson Reuters	Data type: CO2e Scopes 1–3 Time period (years of emissions): from 2002 Total coverage: 7000 companies Includes company-reported data, third-party data, and own estimations.	Mander et al. (2014), Baboukardos (2017)

(continued)

Table 4.1 (continued)

GHG emission data provider	Description	Literature
Sustainalytics	Data type: CO2e Scopes 1–3 Time period (years of emissions): from 2010 Total coverage: 11,000 companies Includes company-reported data, third-party data, and own estimations. Carbon Solutions Suite provides additional information.	Clarkson et al. (2015)
CDP	Data type: CO2e Scopes 1–3 Time period (years of emissions): from 2003 Total coverage: 2000 companies Relies on company-reported data gathered through the CDP questionnaire; no estimations.	Griffin et al. (2017), Depoers et al. (2016), Chen et al. (2021), Ilhan et al. (2023)
Bloomberg	Data type: CO2e Scopes 1–3 Time period (years of emissions): from 2005 Total coverage: 2000 companies Combines data from several sources.	Eccles et al. (2011), Gerged et al. (2021)
Urgentem	Data type: CO2e Scopes 1–3 Time period (years of emissions): over the last 10 years Total coverage: 6000 companies	Giannetti et al. (2023), Carbone et al. (2021), Dunz et al. (2021)
RobecoSAM	The Sustainability Yearbook 2010–2016; survey approach RobecoSAM, a world-famous investment company focusing primarily on global sustainability investing, provides asset management, sustainability assessments, impact analysis and investing, and benchmarking services. It also publishes the Dow Jones Sustainability Indices and The Sustainability Yearbook to rank the sustainability of global companies.	Tan et al. (2020), Billio et al. (2021)

of the goods and services that a company purchases or uses in its operations. Downstream refers to the emissions associated with the distribution, use, and disposal of company's products or services, such as emissions from customers using the products or the waste generated after the product's lifestyle. Both MSCI and CDP provide estimates for all 15 individual scope 3 emission categories. This can be easily aggregated into upstream, downstream, and total scope 3 emissions.

4.2 The Assessment of Climate Risk

Environmental disclosure in banking has become increasingly important due to the rising frequency of natural disasters caused by climate change. Banks are becoming more aware of the growing risk these catastrophic events pose their customers, which could lead to an increase in non-performing loans. For instance, Dal Maso et al. (2022) document that banks in US counties with higher disaster risk recognize larger loan loss provisioning (LLP) after controlling for other bank-level factors related to LLP. Given this empirical evidence, we can confirm that banks are called today to consider climate change risk during the lending process assessment until the time a loan is issued. By 2030, there could be four times the number of heat-waves and twice the number of droughts, and extreme rainstorms could rise by 50%, according to the Intergovernmental Panel on Climate Change. Because banks cannot stop natural disasters, they should assess climate change risk, developing certain resilience and preparing to manage any disaster's post-consequences. In 2015, Mark Carney, governor of the Bank of England and then chairman of the Financial Stability Board (FSB), said: "Climate change will threaten financial resilience and longer-term prosperity." Similarly, the European Central Bank's Financial Stability Review stated, on May 29, 2019, that climate risk may adversely affect the balance sheets of financial institutions, which, therefore, may be relevant for financial stability, particularly if markets are not pricing the related risks correctly. We assist in a new banking era, where addressing climate change has become a critical issue for banks and one of the main priorities for developing their business. As Cortés and Strahan (2017) observed, climate risk matters for banks. They find that multimarket banks reallocate capital after the occurrence of natural disasters because credit demand increases in affected areas. To reduce the impact of the demand shock on credit supply, banks also increase sales of more liquid loans and the interest rate on deposits. An increasing number of banks are claiming heightened awareness of social responsibility as part of their role as financial intermediaries. Indeed, financial market participants and policymakers are increasingly concerned about the potential risks of climate change to economic activity, corporate performance, and asset values. For instance, central banks and regulatory authorities worldwide have begun considering whether climate-related risks might undermine financial stability with adverse economic consequences (EBA/REP/2023/34). Investors are rethinking their strategies and are actively employing ESG-oriented approaches. According to a European Leveraged Finance Association survey from 2019, more than 70% of responding credit managers said they must consider ESG factors in their investment strategies due to increased investor pressure. Moreover, key players in the market have been pulling back investments in environmentally dubious projects. The European Investment Bank has introduced a new energy lending policy banning fossil-fuel financing. Also, central banks recognize the impact of climate change on financial stability. The European Central Bank has recently announced its decision to invest in the Bank for International Settlements' green bond fund, contributing to the world's efforts against climate change. The Green Loan Principles, published by the Loan Market Association in March 2018, provide guidelines for selecting projects as "green." For instance, in January 2020, the Swedish property company Wallenstam obtained a green loan of 258 million dollars to finance a project on creating "nearly zero-energy buildings."

Climate risk is now a top priority for bankers, influencing how they make lending decisions, monitor loans, and manage capital. To empirically capture bank-level exposure to climate risk, we can leverage the study by Sautner et al. (2023), which proposes three proxies based on the bigrams related to climate change occurring in the transcripts of earnings conference calls (see Table 4.2):

Table 4.2 Top 100 bigrams captured by Climate Change Exposure (CCExposure). This lists the top 100 bigrams associated with CCExposure, which measures the relative frequency with which bigrams related to climate change occur in the transcripts of earnings conference calls. Source: Sautner et al. (2023)

Bigram	Frequency	Bigram	Frequency	Bigram	Frequency
Energy	15,605	Solar PV	827	Gas vehicle	560
Electric vehicle	9508	Scale solar	827	Effort energy	560
Clean energy	6430	Need clean	821	Pass house	559
New energy	4544	Coastal area	816	Carbon free	558
Climate change	4374	Energy star	793	Driver assistance	545
Wind power	4253	Environmental footprint	792	Electrical energy	543
Wind energy	4035	Design use	777	Solar installation	541
Energy efficient	3899	Area energy	777	Snow ice	538
Greenhouse gas	3416	Charge station	762	Renewable natural	536
Solar energy	2511	Clean water	759	Promote use	536
Air quality	2409	Major design	747	Farm project	531
Clean air	2301	Vehicle manufacturer	740	Laser diode	528
Carbon emission	2088	Future energy	737	Deliver energy	526
Gas emission	1910	Motor control	726	Protect environment	525
Extreme weather	1773	Combine heat	718	Sustainable energy	523
Carbon dioxide	1583	Electric bus	709	Manage energy	522
Water resource	1423	Distribute power	703	Invest energy	521
Autonomous vehicle	1394	Environmental benefit	695	Electric energy	519
Energy environment	1279	Eco friendly	695	Forest land	512
Wind resource	1245	Electrical vehicle	695	Capacity energy	512
Government India	1201	Carbon neutral	690		
Battery power	1147	Fast charge	675		
Air pollution	1127	Cell power	657		
Battery electric	1121	Energy team	650		
Integrate resource	1052	Cycle gas	646		
Clean power	1008	Coal gasification	643		
Carbon price	999	Environmental concern	643		

(continued)

Table 4.2 (continued)

Bigram	Frequency	Bigram	Frequency	Bigram	Frequency
World population	977	Carbon intensity	641		
Solar farm	971	Energy application	615		
Energy regulatory	967	Produce electricity	604		
Obama administration	957	Help state	604		
Heat power	941	Environmental standard	593		
Carbon tax	928	Power agreement	586		
Unite nation	925	Supply energy	585		
Onshore wind	878	Electric hybrid	585		
Electric motor	869	Source power	575		
Provide energy	851	Sustainability goal	572		
Efficient solution	839	Energy reform	571		
Global warm	837	Plant power	564		
Power generator	828	Compare conventional	560		

(1) *Climate change exposure*, which measures the frequency with which certain climate change bigrams occur in the transcripts of earning calls, scaled by the total number of bigrams in the transcript: they count the number of such bigrams and divide them by the total number of bigrams in the transcripts.
(2) *Climate change risk*, which counts the relative frequency of climate change bigrams mentioned together with the words "risk" or "uncertainty" in one sentence in the transcripts of earnings conference calls.
(3) *Climate change positive sentiment*, such as whether the events represent (in expectation) good news to the firm. The relative frequency with which climate change bigrams are stated together with other positive financial or operational terms could indicate a firm's optimistic outlook on sustainability and its potential for future growth in a green economy.

4.3 ESG Ratings and Data Providers

Environmental disclosure is incorporated into ESG ratings and should be positively related to environmental scores provided by reputable rating agencies (Basu et al., 2022; Christensen et al., 2022). Banks are always under more pressure to consider environmental factors, social welfare, fair labor practices, and nonfinancial dimensions in their activities, mainly in lending. The questions are: Why should banks consider ESG ratings (or scores)? Are these ratings a determinant of their lending strategies? Some reasons can be identified:

(1) In one respect, the bank's own ESG rating may signal its views on ESG-related issues; for example, banks with strong ESG performance tilt toward borrowers with strong ESG ratings.

Alternatively, banks with poor ESG performance may be more interested in repairing their social capital and may, therefore, lean toward borrowers with strong ESG ratings to enhance their image.

(2) A further possibility is that bankers are concerned about their reputation and social capital and fear that the value of this capital may be diminished by doing business with poor ESG-rated borrowers. Reputational concerns about their borrowers could also be incorporated into the structure and pricing of loan agreements as risks that affect the likelihood of debt repayment.

Here, I summarize the main results from the recent empirical literature exploring the role of ESG ratings in banking. For instance, Basu et al. (2022) test whether banks with high ESG ratings (more socially sensible and responsible in providing credit to local communities) originate more home purchase mortgage loans in poor localities than banks with low ESG ratings. This investigation was motivated by the fact that credit market failures and discrimination have historically impeded lending to otherwise creditworthy borrowers in poor neighborhoods. They find that high-ESG banks originate fewer home purchase loans—in both number and dollar amount—annually in poor counties than low-ESG banks. Houston and Shan (2022) find that banks are more likely to grant loans to borrowers with ESG profiles similar to their own and positively influence the borrower's subsequent ESG performance. Abdelsalam et al. (2023) find that banks with higher ESG scores exhibit less procyclical lending behavior than those with lower ESG scores. Therefore, banks with higher ESG scores tend to adopt a more responsible lending model during periods of economic expansion, which curbs their lending volume. Lastly, banks with higher ESG scores adjust their risk strategy to incorporate ESG risk, particularly climate-related risks, which affects their risk appetite and ultimately leads to countercyclical lending (Liu et al., 2024). This aligns with prior studies (Lins et al., 2017; Albuquerque et al., 2020), showing that firms with stronger ESG engagement experience lower downside risks and higher market performance resilience.

The financial crisis of 2008 has severely damaged the reputation of financial institutions. This has forced them to invest considerable resources in rebuilding their reputations and regaining public trust, emphasizing sustainability. The sustainability boost started after the financial crisis, but ESG practices were already on the corporate agenda before the crisis. Thus, some studies focus on how ESG activities impact bank behavior during turbulent times. Cornett et al. (2016) document that banks with higher ESG engagement have better financial performance and stability during crises. Danisman and Tarazi (2024) find that lending falls to a lesser extent for banks with higher ESG scores during crisis times when they consider the global financial crisis of 2007–2009 and the European sovereign debt crisis of 2010–2012. Chiaramonte et al. (2022) find that the total ESG score and its subpillars reduce bank fragility during periods of financial distress. This stabilizing effect holds strongly for banks with higher ESG ratings. However, banks can raise their ESG metrics by telling rosy stories about policies, products, and performance (i.e., greenwashing risk—Lyon & Montgomery, 2015); adding pleasing photos in annual reports, websites, and social media; sponsoring charity programs; selectively disclosing favorable data; and, more recently, underwriting or issuing ESG-labeled instruments, like green bonds. For instance, green bonds (i.e., bonds with a use-of-proceeds requirement toward environmental projects) have evolved into a significant asset class that reputable and visible companies frequently employ to finance their sustainability strategies (e.g., Flammer, 2021; Lu, 2021; Baker et al., 2022; Bedendo et al., 2023). Moreover, large banks, arguably under greater pressure from stakeholders to legitimize their operations and lending choices, are particularly inclined to boost their environmental profiles. However, they provide large amounts of credit to "brown" borrowers. Banks are also not particularly incentivized to cut this relationship with brown borrowers in the presence of mandatory sustainability reporting and external auditors (Kacperczyk & Peydró, 2022; Ivanov et al., 2022; Giannetti et al., 2023). Today, we still observe that undercapitalized banks are more likely to finance brown firms in trouble, emphasizing a zombie phenomenon (Peek & Rosengren, 2005; Caballero et al., 2008; Giannetti & Simonov, 2013; Acharya et al., 2019; Fontana & Longo, 2022). This phenomenon indicates a sort of dangerous banking fragility, leading to low financial stability.

Between ESG data providers, divergence and competition could lead to higher quality (Berg et al., 2022). Academics are the first to have concerns about the quality and accuracy of these ESG ratings (e.g., Larcker et al., 2022). Today, the main ESG data providers used in empirical economic studies are MSCI KLD, Bloomberg, ISS, Refinitiv (Asset4), and S&P Global (RobecoSAM). Some of these providers offer detailed GHG emission data, as mentioned in Sect. 4.1. In the following table (Table 4.3), I summarize the characteristics of the most used ESG data sources in banking studies to identify ESG practices in lending.

Table 4.3 Summary of the main ESG data providers used in banking literature

ESG data provider	Description	Literature
Refinitiv ASSET4	Content research analysts calculate these scores trained to collect ESG data, and they are based on publicly reported company-level data, such as annual company reports and corporate social responsibility reports, stock exchange filings, and the news media. The scores are grouped into ten categories, forming the three pillar scores (environment, social, and governance) and the combined score.	Hauptmann (2017), He et al. (2021), Danisman and Tarazi (2024), Chiaramonte et al. (2022), Ersoy et al. (2022), Basu et al. (2022)

(continued)

Table 4.3 Continued

ESG data provider	Description	Literature
MSCI KLD	Morgan Stanley Capital International (MSCI) ESG database (formerly known as Kinder, Lyndenberg, and Domini Research and Analytics Inc. (KLD) database) is one of the most prominent ESG rating agencies. KLD coverage has expanded over time. It began with roughly 650 unique firms in the 1990s and increased to over 1000 by 2001. Except for the most recent years, it does not provide data on European countries.	Erhemjamts et al. (2024), Basu et al. (2022)
Bloomberg	The Bloomberg terminal provides our ESG data. Bloomberg collects, scrubs, verifies, and continually updates environmental, social, and governance (ESG) data from published company disclosures. The database currently covers approximately 9500 companies from 83 different countries.	Azmi et al. (2021), Blundell-Wignall and Roulet (2013), Basu et al. (2022)
Sustainalytics	Sustainalytics is a leading independent ESG rating provider (later acquired by Morningstar, Inc.) that assigns sustainability-related KPIs in loan agreements.	Kim et al. (2022)
RepRisk	The RepRisk data provide a monthly unbroken time-series ESG rating and coverage of negative ESG news. RepRisk does not cover positive ESG events. Part of the reason can be attributed to positive news being more likely to be self-reported for branding and marketing purposes and subject to greenwashing biases.	Houston and Shan (2022), Hrazdil et al. (2023), He et al. (2021), Anginer et al. (2020), Becchetti and Manfredonia (2022)
FactSet Truvalue Labs	TVL, relatively novel, is a San Francisco-based artificial intelligence (AI)/big data company that processes unstructured data from 100,000+ non-company-reported (i.e., non-self-reported) sources through natural language processing (NLP) in providing continuous updates for quantifiable ESG sentiment information toward firms along 26 ESG concerns.	Erhemjamts et al. (2024)

4.4 ESG Disclosure: Regulatory Insights

Banks have been affected by increased ESG disclosure mandates since they are large multinational companies operating in many countries and playing an important economic role in supporting economic growth. The transition from voluntary environmental disclosure to mandated disclosure represents a paradigm change, where banks must use and produce accurate information regarding green aspects. Thus, ESG disclosure regulations require firms to provide information about the environmental and social (E&S) impacts of their operating, investing, and financing activities, meeting the regulatory criteria (e.g., size threshold, listing status).

Financial supervisors and policymakers have recognized the importance of disclosing and assessing climate-related financial risks. Legislators in the European Union (EU) have been pioneers in addressing climate change, emphasizing the stewardship role of banks for the transition and calling for greater transparency of financial institutions' environmental impact (e.g., European Commission, 2018; UN Environment Programme Finance Initiative, 2022). For instance, the European Union had already endorsed in 2014 the Non-Financial Reporting Directive (NFRD 2014/95/EU), requiring large companies with more than 500 employees to report on sustainability-related themes such as environment, social, and employee issues; human rights; bribery; and corruption (Hummel & Jobst, 2023). It requires the companies to disclose implemented due diligence processes, business models, risk management, and key performance indicators relevant to the business. The trend is to produce rules dedicated only to the banking sector in the future, affecting less equally large financial and nonfinancial companies. A valid regulatory example comes from Ireland's 2008 Credit Institutions Act, which explicitly requires all Irish banks to issue biannual corporate responsibility reports.

A further consideration regarding the shift from voluntary to mandatory disclosure is driven by the trade-off that firms face when deciding whether it is convenient to disclose or not. This is generally valid, as emphasized in the second chapter of this monograph, which is dedicated to the cost-benefit relation of disclosing.

In the context of climate change, disclosing climate risks may expose sensitive information about firm's future strategy. However, mandatory ESG disclosures can have positive, real-world impacts. Christensen et al. (2021), highlight the effects of disclosure on mine safety records in financial reports, while Bonetti et al. (2023) examine disclosures related to hydraulic fracking fluids. Despite some skepticism about the validity of mandatory environmental and social (E&S) disclosures - mainly due to the standardized nature of the reporting - reliable, audited information in the banking industry can alleviate concerns. Supervisory validation helps ensure the accuracy of disclosures, reducing the risk of greenwashing and ensuring transparency.

Here, I sum up the main regulatory events dedicated to the EU banking industry requiring E&S disclosure and climate risk considerations:

- Adoption of the Disclosure Directive: European Union (EU) policymakers adopted the Disclosure Directive in 2014, requiring member states to mandate listed companies, banks, and certain financial groups to disclose nonfinancial information to the market, including environmental sustainability risks and related environmental sustainability information concerning renewable and non-renewable energy, land use, water use, air pollution, greenhouse gas emissions, and the use of hazardous materials. The disclosure requirement applies only to large listed credit institutions and large listed insurance companies that are the parent companies of a large group. These organizations must have an average of more than 500 employees, based on the group's consolidated total.
- Publication of a European Systemic Risk Board (ESRB) paper: in 2016, the ESRB published a paper recommending policy actions to address the potential

systemic risk of transitioning to a more environmentally sustainable and green economy; this could involve short-term and medium-term regulatory measures. A short-term regulatory response would heavily rely on a better understanding of (i) banks' and other connected financial firms' direct exposures to nonfinancial firms with immediate, emerging, and elevated environmental risks and (ii) the consequences of a disorderly transition to a low-carbon economy. For example, enhanced disclosure of bank exposures to sustainability risks would facilitate a timely assessment of potential risks to financial stability and promote a "smooth rather than an abrupt transition toward a lower-carbon economy."

- Publication of the Task Force on Climate-Related Financial Disclosures (TCFD) report: in June 2017, FSB's industry-led TFCD published its final report containing recommendations for improving principles and practices for voluntary corporate disclosures that can promote a "smooth rather than an abrupt transition towards a lower-carbon economy." The TCFD consisted of representatives from the private sector, including investors, information preparers, and other market participants from various industries and regions. They recommended that all listed companies, including banks and financial institutions, make certain disclosures to investors about (i) the governance of climate risks within their institutions, (ii) their strategy for dealing with it, (iii) their risk management approach, and (iv) the targets and metrics they use.
- The 2019 revision of the Capital Requirements package: this incorporates climate change risks within the three pillars of bank supervision.
- Coming into force of the Green Taxonomy: this regulation came into force in 2020. For economic activity to count as green (be "Taxonomy aligned"), it must substantially contribute to at least one of the EU's environmental objectives, not harm any other objectives, and comply with global governance standards. The EU's Platform on Sustainable Finance has developed detailed technical screening criteria for over 100 activities to determine whether they contribute to climate change mitigation and adaptation.
- Incorporation of ESG risk across the pillars of EU bank supervision:

(1) Pillar I: Regulatory capital requirement—the assessment of dedicated prudential treatment of exposures related to assets or activities associated substantially with environmental and social objectives (under the responsibility of the European Banking Authority (EBA) by 28 June 2025, though it was initially anticipated to be in 2023 according to the 2021 Sustainable Finance Strategy (n. 31))

(2) Pillar II: Supervision—ESG risk definition, proposals on ESG risk assessment methodologies, and the feasibility of incorporating ESG risks into the supervisory review and evaluation process (SREP) (EBA, delivered on 23 June 2021)

(3) Pillar III: Disclosures—mandatory (biannual) disclosure of ESG risks following the EBA Pillar III report (EBA, European Commission EBA standards published in January 2022, application delayed to end in 2023)

Despite the efforts, the trajectory of existing EU sustainable finance regulation is still unclear and not well coordinated with supervisory requirements. Policymakers have ambiguous objectives, and their approach is still weak to translate environmental factors into financial risks. There is some evidence that large banks are taking ESG risks on board as part of internal governance arrangements. One study of large European banks finds that they all discuss ESG topics in board committee meetings, and nine out of 24 have a risk committee dedicated to this topic (de Sá, 2022). To conclude, the path toward sustainable banking in the EU still presents much room for reaching the goal.

4.5 Green Lending: Pricing Effect and Dedicated Instruments

Bank loans represent banks' most important source of profits and financing for many companies. Therefore, a strong understanding of the underlying relationship provides insightful information on how the power of banks can be leveraged to drive sustainability; given their role as key drivers of the economy, banks have become one of the focal points of sustainable climate investments as the transition to a lower-carbon economy requires significant private capital to be mobilized over the next couple of decades. In the past, banks have viewed climate change through the lens of corporate social responsibility (CSR), focusing on their responsibilities as "corporate citizens" to safeguard their reputations. More recently, banks' focus has expanded to incorporate the possibility of increased credit risk induced by the severity of climate change. Delis et al. (2019) examine the risk of fossil fuel reserves becoming "stranded" when transitioning to a low-carbon economy and losing economic value. They find that in the post-Paris Agreement period, banks have increased the cost of borrowing by 16 bps for fossil fuel firms with proven reserves. Kleimeier and Viehs (2015) show that firms that voluntarily disclose their carbon emissions through the Carbon Disclosure Project survey have a lower cost of debt than their non-disclosing counterparts. Adverse climate incidents can affect the pricing and terms of loan contracts through two channels (Hauptmann, 2017):

- The first is credit risk. Adverse climate incidents can reveal information about client firms' climate-related risks and the risk-management processes in place to mitigate such risks. These risks can significantly affect the level and uncertainty of a firm's future cash flows, which can affect the firm's ability to repay its loans and the value of the collateral that could be recovered in the event of default.
- The second is reputational risk. Banks face reputational risks from the possibility of being associated with a client firm's climate scandal and may require a premium to enter into a lending relationship with a firm that the public and the banks' other stakeholders may view as having socially questionable climate practices.

Even without higher credit risk, banks may face reputational risk when they associate themselves with polluting firms or firms perceived as environmentally irresponsible by the public or the banks' stakeholders. Corporate reputation and reputational risk have become increasingly relevant for firms because of the growing prominence of social media, where bad news spreads quickly. Moreover, as public concern about climate change has increased, there has been growing pressure from the public for financial institutions to practice responsible lending. Companies experiencing an adverse climate event will receive less favorable loan terms. The empirical literature agrees, showing an increase in loan spreads from 13 to 52 basis points relative to pre-event spreads. This effect becomes more severe with the events' intensity and influence (Hauptmann, 2017; Hrazdil et al., 2023). There are also indirect economic costs associated with climate incidents. These include the negative perceptions held by employees, customers, suppliers, and other stakeholders and a detrimental impact on the firm's ability to recruit and employ a more talented and committed workforce. In recent years, ESG lending activity around the world has grown exponentially. The proliferation drives this growth of use-of-proceeds-based green loans and general-purpose sustainability-linked loans (SLLs). Green loans are similar to green bonds because their proceeds should be entirely used to finance green projects. In contrast to green loans, sustainable loans do not restrict the use of proceeds; i.e., financing could be utilized for general corporate needs.

For instance, Dursun-de Neef et al. (2023) find that green loans motivate firms to shrink their environmental emissions; however, their social performance deteriorates. Sustainable loans, on the other hand, incentivize firms to improve their ESG performance by increasing their environmental and governance scores. These results show that sustainable loans might be a more efficient instrument to enhance firms' overall ESG performance. In particular, SLLs represent one of the most rapidly expanding segments within sustainable finance, aiming to encourage borrowers to meet preestablished sustainability performance targets. These loans are issued between reputable firms and banks with superior ESG profiles that face greater stakeholder scrutiny, mostly as revolving credit facilities through banking relationships. Although SLLs have become the predominant source of ESG-contingent financing for firms over the past decade, the widespread use of these loans has also raised questions regarding greenwashing in this market due to concerns about ESG transparency.

The key role of financial intermediation in sustainability economics is undoubtedly important. Indeed, banks can drive the economy toward emission neutrality (Ehlers et al., 2022; Delis et al., 2019; Tran et al., 2021; Gao et al., 2021). A further question arises whether banks involved in this sustainable transition can still be profitable. For instance, Del Gaudio et al. (2022) find that a higher propensity to green lending is associated with lower profitability, more moderate default risk, and lower credit risk than banks with a less green investment approach. Traditionally, the banking sector's profitability has been explained through two main theories: the market power hypothesis and the efficiency hypothesis. The market power hypothesis considers that greater market concentration or market share facilitates setting higher prices for customers, thereby increasing extraordinary profit. The efficiency hypothesis suggests that more efficient banks have lower unit costs, which allows them to attract more customers. Lower unit costs would allow setting lower interest rates for loans and higher interest rates for deposits. Sustainable business models can boost market share because socially and environmentally responsible actions improve reputation, confidence, and customer loyalty. This loyalty is important in the banking sector since high competition and customer relationships represent an appetite portfolio for the rivals.

When we think about banks grounded on sustainability as the mainstream of their business, we guess that sustainable banks are less concerned with short-term profit maximization and are oriented toward maximizing stakeholder value and client satisfaction by decreasing the harmful effects of economic activities on the environment and society. However, sustainable banks could risk losing efficiency if they put too much emphasis on social and environmental investments. Furthermore, trying to satisfy all stakeholders could adversely affect profitability due to the inefficient use of resources. We have learned from the prior literature that banks are more than ever obliged to take care of climate risk and provide and use accurate environmental information to protect financial stability. In this way, they can mitigate risk exposure and contain the amount of nonperforming portfolios. Financing brown (instead of green) industries could still be one issue to accept in the transition to a more eco-friendly economy (Kacperczyk & Peydró, 2022). Today, banks run the risk of being more overwhelmed by financial diseases and scandals of brown borrowers than green ones. Literature has highlighted the challenge of identifying borrowers who appears to be "green" but my actually be "brown" due to greenwashing risks. This makes it difficult for banks to detect these risks early enough to take appropriate action.

References

Abdelsalam, O., Azmi, W., Disli, M., & Kowsalya, V. (2023). Bank lending cyclicality and ESG activities: Global evidence. *Finance Research Letters, 58*, 104541.

Acharya, V. V., Eisert, T., Eufinger, C., & Hirsch, C. (2019). Whatever it takes: The real effects of unconventional monetary policy. *The Review of Financial Studies, 32*(9), 3366–3411.

Aintablian, S., Mcgraw, P. A., & Roberts, G. S. (2007). Bank monitoring and environmental risk. *Journal of Business Finance & Accounting, 34*(1-2), 389–401.

Albuquerque, R., Brandão-Marques, L., Ferreira, M. A., & Matos, P. (2019). International corporate governance spillovers: Evidence from cross-border mergers and acquisitions. *The Review of Financial Studies, 32*(2), 738–770.

Albuquerque, R., Koskinen, Y., Yang, S., & Zhang, C. (2020). Resiliency of environmental and social stocks: An analysis of the exogenous COVID-19 market crash. *The Review of Corporate Finance Studies, 9*(3), 593–621.

Anginer, D., Hrazdil, K., Li, J., & Zhang, R. (2020). Adverse climate incidents and bank loan contracting. *Available at SSRN 3723771*.

Aswani, J., Raghunandan, A., & Rajgopal, S. (2024). Are carbon emissions associated with stock returns? *Review of Finance, 28*(1), 75–106.

Azar, J., Duro, M., Kadach, I., & Ormazabal, G. (2021). The big three and corporate carbon emissions around the world. *Journal of Financial Economics, 142*(2), 674–696.

Azmi, W., Hassan, M. K., Houston, R., & Karim, M. S. (2021). ESG activities and banking performance: International evidence from emerging economies. *Journal of International Financial Markets, Institutions and Money, 70*, 101277.

Baboukardos, D. (2017, September). Market valuation of greenhouse gas emissions under a mandatory reporting regime: Evidence from the UK. In *Accounting forum* (Vol. 41, No. 3, pp. 221–233). No longer published by Elsevier.

Baker, M., Bergstresser, D., Serafeim, G., & Wurgler, J. (2022). The pricing and ownership of US green bonds. *Annual Review of Financial Economics, 14*, 415–437.

Baldini, J. U., Bertram, R. A., & Ridley, H. E. (2018). Ground air: A first approximation of the Earth's second largest reservoir of carbon dioxide gas. *Science of the Total Environment, 616*, 1007–1013.

Basu, S., Vitanza, J., Wang, W., & Zhu, X. R. (2022). Walking the walk? Bank ESG disclosures and home mortgage lending. *Review of Accounting Studies, 27*(3), 779–821.

Becchetti, L., & Manfredonia, S. (2022). Media, reputational risk, and bank loan contracting. *Journal of Financial Stability, 60*, 100990.

Bedendo, M., Nocera, G., & Siming, L. (2023). Greening the financial sector: Evidence from bank green bonds. *Journal of Business Ethics, 188*(2), 259–279.

Berg, F., Koelbel, J. F., & Rigobon, R. (2022). Aggregate confusion: The divergence of ESG ratings. *Review of Finance, 26*(6), 1315–1344.

Berthelot, S., Cormier, D., & Magnan, M. (2003). Environmental, disclosure research: Review and synthesis. *Journal of Accounting Literature, 22*(1), 1–44.

Billio, M., Costola, M., Hristova, I., Latino, C., & Pelizzon, L. (2021). Inside the ESG ratings: (Dis) agreement and performance. *Corporate Social Responsibility and Environmental Management, 28*(5), 1426–1445.

Blundell-Wignall, A., & Roulet, C. (2013). Bank lending puzzles: Business models and the responsiveness to policy. *OECD Journal: Financial Market Trends, 2013*(1), 7–30.

Bolton, P., & Kacperczyk, M. (2021). Do investors care about carbon risk? *Journal of Financial Economics, 142*(2), 517–549.

Bonacchi, M., Klein, A., Longo, S., & Strampelli, G. (2022). The effects of credible voluntary disclosures: Institutional investor engagement and investees' ESG performances. *European Corporate Governance Institute-Law Working Paper*, (622).

Bonetti, P., Leuz, C., & Michelon, G. (2023). *Internalizing externalities: Disclosure regulation for hydraulic fracturing, drilling activity and water quality* (No. w30842). National Bureau of Economic Research.

Busch, T., Johnson, M., & Pioch, T. (2022). Corporate carbon performance data: Quo vadis? *Journal of Industrial Ecology, 26*(1), 350–363.

Caballero, R. J., Hoshi, T., & Kashyap, A. K. (2008). Zombie lending and depressed restructuring in Japan. *American Economic Review, 98*(5), 1943–1977.

Carbone, S., Giuzio, M., Kapadia, S., Krämer, J. S., Nyholm, K., & Vozian, K. (2021). The low-carbon transition, climate commitments and firm credit risk.

Chen, F., Hussain, M., Khan, J. A., Mir, G. M., & Khan, Z. (2021). Voluntary disclosure of greenhouse gas emissions by cities under carbon disclosure project: A sustainable development approach. *Sustainable Development, 29*(4), 719–727.

Chiaramonte, L., Dreassi, A., Girardone, C., & Piserà, S. (2022). Do ESG strategies enhance bank stability during financial turmoil? Evidence from Europe. *The European Journal of Finance, 28*(12), 1173–1211.

Christensen, D. M., Serafeim, G., & Sikochi, A. (2022). Why is corporate virtue in the eye of the beholder? The case of ESG ratings. *The Accounting Review, 97*(1), 147–175.

Christensen, H. B., Hail, L., & Leuz, C. (2021). Mandatory CSR and sustainability reporting: Economic analysis and literature review. *Review of Accounting Studies, 26*(3), 1176–1248.

Clarkson, P. M., Li, Y., Pinnuck, M., & Richardson, G. D. (2015). The valuation relevance of greenhouse gas emissions under the European Union carbon emissions trading scheme. *European Accounting Review, 24*(3), 551–580.

Cohen, S., Kadach, I., & Ormazabal, G. (2023). Institutional investors, climate disclosure, and carbon emissions. *Journal of Accounting and Economics, 76*(2–3), 101640.

Cornett, M. M., Erhemjamts, O., & Tehranian, H. (2016). Greed or good deeds: An examination of the relation between corporate social responsibility and the financial performance of US commercial banks around the financial crisis. *Journal of Banking & Finance, 70*, 137–159.

Cortés, K. R., & Strahan, P. E. (2017). Tracing out capital flows: How financially integrated banks respond to natural disasters. *Journal of Financial Economics, 125*(1), 182–199.

Dal Maso, L., Kanagaretnam, K., Lobo, G. J., & Mazzi, F. (2022). Does disaster risk relate to banks' loan loss provisions? *European Accounting Review*, 1–30.

Danisman, G. O., & Tarazi, A. (2024). ESG activity and bank lending during financial crises. *Journal of Financial Stability, 70*, 101206.

de Sá, M. (2022). ESG and Banks: Towards Sustainable Banking in the European Union. In *The Palgrave Handbook of ESG and Corporate Governance* (pp. 375–398). Springer International Publishing.

Del Gaudio, B. L., Previtali, D., Sampagnaro, G., Verdoliva, V., & Vigne, S. (2022). Syndicated green lending and lead bank performance. *Journal of International Financial Management & Accounting, 33*(3), 412–427.

Delis, M. D., De Greiff, K., & Ongena, S. (2019). Being stranded with fossil fuel reserves? Climate policy risk and the pricing of bank loans. *Climate Policy Risk and the Pricing of Bank loans (September 10, 2019). EBRD Working Paper*, (231).

Depoers, F., Jeanjean, T., & Jérôme, T. (2016). Voluntary disclosure of greenhouse gas emissions: Contrasting the carbon disclosure project and corporate reports. *Journal of Business Ethics, 134*, 445–461.

Dhaliwal, D. S., Li, O. Z., Tsang, A., & Yang, Y. G. (2011). Voluntary nonfinancial disclosure and the cost of equity capital: The initiation of corporate social responsibility reporting. *The Accounting Review, 86*(1), 59–100.

Dunz, N., Emambakhsh, T., Hennig, T., Kaijser, M., Kouratzoglou, C., & Salleo, C. (2021). ECB's Economy-Wide Climate Stress Test. *ECB Occasional Paper*, (2021/281).

Dursun-de Neef, Ö., Ongena, S., & Tsonkova, G. (2023). Green versus sustainable loans: The impact on firms' ESG performance. *Swiss Finance Institute Research Paper*, (22-42).

Eccles, R. G., Serafeim, G., & Krzus, M. P. (2011). Market interest in nonfinancial information. *Journal of Applied Corporate Finance, 23*(4), 113–127.

Ehlers, T., Packer, F., & De Greiff, K. (2022). The pricing of carbon risk in syndicated loans: Which risks are priced and why? *Journal of Banking & Finance, 136*, 106180.

Erhemjamts, O., Huang, K., & Tehranian, H. (2024). Climate risk, ESG performance, and ESG sentiment in US commercial banks. *Global Finance Journal, 59*, 100924.

Ersoy, E., Swiecka, B., Grima, S., Özen, E., & Romanova, I. (2022). The impact of ESG scores on bank market value? Evidence from the US banking industry. *Sustainability, 14*(15), 9527.

Flammer, C. (2021). Corporate green bonds. *Journal of Financial Economics, 142*(2), 499–516.

Fontana, S., & Longo, S. (2022). Azienda familiare e la crisi di impresa. In *La valutazione delle aziende familiari* (pp. 41–55). Giuffrè.

Gao, H., Ru, H., & Tang, D. Y. (2021). Subnational debt of China: The politics-finance nexus. *Journal of Financial Economics, 141*(3), 881–895.

Gerged, A. M., Matthews, L., & Elheddad, M. (2021). Mandatory disclosure, greenhouse gas emissions and the cost of equity capital: UK evidence of a U-shaped relationship. *Business Strategy and the Environment, 30*(2), 908–930.

Giannetti, M., Jasova, M., Loumioti, M., & Mendicino, C. (2023). "Glossy Green" Banks: The Disconnect Between Environmental Disclosures and Lending Activities.

Giannetti, M., & Simonov, A. (2013). On the real effects of bank bailouts: Micro evidence from Japan. *American Economic Journal: Macroeconomics, 5*(1), 135–167.

Grewal, J., & Serafeim, G. (2020). Research on corporate sustainability: Review and directions for future research. *Foundations and Trends® in Accounting, 14*(2), 73–127.

Griffin, P. A., Lont, D. H., & Sun, E. Y. (2017). The relevance to investors of greenhouse gas emission disclosures. *Contemporary Accounting Research, 34*(2), 1265–1297.

Gurvich, A., & Creamer, G. G. (2021). Overallocation and correction of carbon emissions in the evaluation of carbon footprint. *Sustainability, 13*(24), 13613.

Hasan, I., He, Q., & Lu, H. (2022). Social capital, trusting, and trustworthiness: Evidence from peer-to-peer lending. *Journal of Financial and Quantitative Analysis, 57*(4), 1409–1453.

Hauptmann, C. (2017). Corporate sustainability performance and bank loan pricing: It pays to be good, but only when banks are too. *Saïd Business School WP, 20.*

He, R., Chen, X., Chen, C., Zhai, J., & Cui, L. (2021). Environmental, social, and governance incidents and bank loan contracts. *Sustainability, 13*(4), 1885.

Hooks, J., & van Staden, C. J. (2011). Evaluating environmental disclosures: The relationship between quality and extent measures. *The British Accounting Review, 43*(3), 200–213.

Houston, J. F., & Shan, H. (2022). Corporate ESG profiles and banking relationships. *The Review of Financial Studies, 35*(7), 3373–3417.

Hrazdil, K., Anginer, D., Li, J., & Zhang, R. (2023). Climate reputation and bank loan contracting. *Journal of Business Ethics*, 1–22.

Hummel, K., & Jobst, D. (2023). Does mandatory sustainability reporting decrease loan costs?. *Available at SSRN 4641046.*

Ilhan, E., Krueger, P., Sautner, Z., & Starks, L. T. (2023). Climate risk disclosure and institutional investors. *The Review of Financial Studies, 36*(7), 2617–2650.

Ioannou, I., & Serafeim, G. (2012). What drives corporate social performance? The role of nation-level institutions. *Journal of International Business Studies, 43*, 834–864.

Ioannou, I., & Serafeim, G. (2017). The consequences of mandatory corporate sustainability reporting. *Harvard Business School research working paper*, (11-100).

Ivanov, I. T., Macchiavelli, M., & Santos, J. A. (2022). Bank lending networks and the propagation of natural disasters. *Financial Management, 51*(3), 903–927.

Kacperczyk, M. T., & Peydró, J. L. (2022). Carbon emissions and the bank-lending channel. *Available at SSRN 3915486.*

Kim, S., Kumar, N., Lee, J., & Oh, J. (2022). ESG lending. In *Proceedings of Paris December 2021 Finance Meeting EUROFIDAI-ESSEC, European Corporate Governance Institute–Finance Working Paper* (No. 817).

Kleimeier, S., & Viehs, M. (2015). CO2 disclosure cuts the cost of debt. *Principles for Responsible Investment: PRI Academic Network RI Quarterly, 7*, 11–12.

Korca, B., Costa, E., & Farneti, F. (2021). From voluntary to mandatory non-financial disclosure following Directive 2014/95/EU: An Italian case study. *Accounting in Europe, 18*(3), 353–377.

Larcker, D. F., Pomorski, L., Tayan, B., & Watts, E. M. (2022). ESG ratings: A Compass without direction. *Rock Center for Corporate Governance at Stanford University Working Paper Forthcoming.*

Lins, K. V., Servaes, H., & Tamayo, A. (2017). Social capital, trust, and firm performance: The value of corporate social responsibility during the financial crisis. *The Journal of Finance, 72*(4), 1785–1824.

Liu, J., Ge, Z., & Wang, Y. (2024). Role of environmental, social, and governance rating data in predicting financial risk and risk management. *Corporate Social Responsibility and Environmental Management, 31*(1), 260–273.

Loew, E., Klein, D., & Pavicevac, A. (2019). Corporate Social Responsibility Reports of European Banks–An Empirical Analysis of the Disclosure Quality and its Determinants.

Lu, S. S. (2021). *The green bonding hypothesis: How do green bonds enhance the credibility of environmental commitments?* Doctoral dissertation, The University of Chicago.

Lyon, T. P., & Montgomery, A. W. (2015). The means and end of greenwash. *Organization & Environment, 28*(2), 223–249.

Mander, Ü., Dotro, G., Ebie, Y., Towprayoon, S., Chiemchaisri, C., Nogueira, S. F., Jamsranjav, B., Kasak, K., Truu, J., Tournebize, J., & Mitsch, W. J. (2014). Greenhouse gas emission in constructed wetlands for wastewater treatment: A review. *Ecological Engineering, 66*, 19–35.

Nguyen, Q., Diaz-Rainey, I., Kitto, A., McNeil, B. I., Pittman, N. A., & Zhang, R. (2023). Scope 3 emissions: Data quality and machine learning prediction accuracy. *PLOS Climate, 2*(11), e0000208.

Peek, J., & Rosengren, E. S. (2005). Unnatural selection: Perverse incentives and the misallocation of credit in Japan. *American Economic Review, 95*(4), 1144–1166.

Sautner, Z., Van Lent, L., Vilkov, G., & Zhang, R. (2023). Firm-level climate change exposure. *The Journal of Finance, 78*(3), 1449–1498.

Schiemann, F., & Sakhel, A. (2019). Carbon disclosure, contextual factors, and information asymmetry: The case of physical risk reporting. *European Accounting Review, 28*(4), 791–818.

Schröder, P. (2022). Mandatory non-financial reporting in the banking industry: Assessing reporting quality and determinants. *Cogent Business & Management, 9*(1), 2073628.

Serafeim, G. (2020). Public sentiment and the price of corporate sustainability. *Financial Analysts Journal, 76*(2), 26–46.

Swinkels, L., & Markwat, T. (2024). Corporate carbon emissions data for equity and bond portfolios. *Managerial Finance, 50*(1), 118–139.

Tan, Y., Shuai, C., Shen, L., Hou, L., & Zhang, G. (2020). A study of sustainable practices in the sustainability leadership of international contractors. *Sustainable Development, 28*(4), 697–710.

Thompson, P., & Cowton, C. J. (2004). Bringing the environment into bank lending: Implications for environmental reporting. *The British Accounting Review, 36*(2), 197–218.

Tran, D. V., Hassan, M. K., Alam, A. W., Pezzo, L., & Abdul-Majid, M. (2021). Economic policy uncertainty, agency problem, and funding structure: Evidence from US banking industry. *Research in International Business and Finance, 58*, 101470.

Veltri, S., Cristiano, E., & Ferraro, O. (2023). Examining the quality of the consolidated mandatory non-financial statements of a cooperative banking group: A longitudinal analysis. *Corporate Social Responsibility and Environmental Management, 30*(4), 1573–1587.

Wang, J., Ma, M., Dong, T., & Zhang, Z. (2023). Do ESG ratings promote corporate green innovation? A quasi-natural experiment based on SynTao Green Finance's ESG ratings. *International Review of Financial Analysis, 87*, 102623.

Xing, C., Zhang, Y., & Tripe, D. (2021). Green credit policy and corporate access to bank loans in China: The role of environmental disclosure and green innovation. *International Review of Financial Analysis, 77*, 101838.

Chapter 5
Do Transparent Banks Do More Green Lending? Evidence from Climate Stress Tests

5.1 Aim and Motivation of the Empirical Investigation

This chapter empirically analyses the impact of one of the first climate stress tests conducted by a central bank on bank lending practices, specifically examining how it influences the volume of green and sustainability-linked loans. Based on prior literature, concerning the positive and negative effects of stress test disclosure (see Chap. 3, Sect. 3.4), I consider the unprecedented experience of the recent climate stress tests in the Euro area. The first time was in 2020, when the European Banking Authority (EBA) decided to conduct an EU-wide pilot exercise to map banks' climate risk. Generally, climate stress tests are an important tool to enforce the broad regulation requiring banks to consider borrowers' environmental information in their lending decision process, showing whether and how they have implemented their risk models within the new climate change risk. Central banks, particularly the EBA and the European Central Bank (ECB), have proactively addressed EU banks during these last years, requiring them to assume a responsibility toward a green economy. As noted by Ellahie (2013) and Fernandes et al. (2020), supervisory tools, like stress tests, have gained more credibility from the perspectives of market participants. Undoubtedly, the context under which banks are called to a stress test increases the complexity of the scenario analysis. As mentioned, banks often lack transparency in their strategies for achieving goals and addressing challenges. However, if banks provide opaque information to markets, they are also the first to collect unclear information from their borrowers. The reliability of this information trembles when there is no validation from an auditing company, especially concerning nonfinancial information. This often happens in the case of small and medium enterprises, which represent most borrowers for large commercial banks. Today, financial and nonfinancial information is fundamental to the lending decision process of a lender. The quality of this information can affect the conditions of an issued loan, e.g., pricing linked to the interest rate, fees and commissions, the

© The Author(s), under exclusive license to Springer Nature Switzerland AG 2025

S. Longo, *Disclosure in Banking*, SIDREA Series in Accounting and Business Administration, https://doi.org/10.1007/978-3-031-84196-5_5

payment plan, and the possibility of revising the same conditions in the long run. Therefore, green lending has become increasingly important due to the banking industry's role in supporting the transition to a decarbonized economy. Green lending is based on two types of loans: green and sustainability-linked loans. Given the details in the prior chapter (Chap. 4) on the main differences between these two kinds of loans (particularly if the financing process is linked to a green project—i.e., green loans), the common factor in both cases is that banks should consider borrowers' nonfinancial information, particularly environmental disclosures. Whether transparency can reduce the uncertainty of a bank's climate risk exposure by increasing its confidence to do more green lending remains an open question. In this case, we can predict that if a bank transparently discloses its climate exposure through central bank scrutiny, it will be better positioned to avoid financing high-risk "brown" industries and instead prioritize "green" borrowers, thereby minimizing potential credit losses related to climate risks. Contrary to this, we could expect that a transparent bank disclosing its climate risk exposure (under the climate stress test) might decide to reduce the future amount of green lending because the greenwashing risk (transferred from borrowers' environmental disclosure) is damaging its reputation. Prior studies on stress test disclosure transparency are ambiguous. Here, another element, according to prior experiences with stress tests, is the complexity of reading and measuring climate risk in a scenario analysis due to the uncertainty of adverse events. This empirical study is crucial because banks are now required to consider new risks in their lending practices, and at the same time, they are adapting how they manage transparency, often relying on borrowers to provide the necessary information.

5.2 Climate Stress Test: Which Risks Do Banks Have to Consider?

There is an urgency to find a good estimation of the impact of climate risks on financial systems, and climate policy timing matters. The banking financial risks stemming from climate change are mainly physical and transition risks, as well as regulatory and reputational risks (Huang et al., 2021). These risks should nowadays be considered by banks since they can significantly affect the level and uncertainty of borrowers' future cash flows, which can impact the ability to repay loans and the value of collateral that could be recovered in the event of default. Transition risks are the most debated since they could arise if much more stringent climate policies are implemented by regulators and supervisors at both national and international levels. The climate transition exposure for a bank consists of identifying the absolute amount of loans to the fossil-fuel sector. Reports usually provide static exposure without quantifying losses the banks could bear under different transition pathways. To gain such insights, transition risk assessment needs to be conducted based on forward-looking scenarios (Battiston, 2019). One way to achieve this is climate stress testing, which has emerged as a state-of-the-art tool in prior climate finance studies (Battiston et al., 2017; Battiston & Monasterolo, 2019; Reinders et al., 2023). Climate change differs significantly from the most commonly modeled "traditional" shocks. The dangers of climate change are also referred to as "risk," but the phenomenon carries much more uncertainty than normal. Atmospheric and environmental impacts are extremely complex and have a multifaceted correlation with human activities.

A common consideration is that today, there is a notable gap between the policies' objectives in decarbonizing the economy and the methodologies to apply in climate stress test exercises (Battiston et al., 2017). Researchers have proposed several methods to measure the climate exposure of a bank. For instance, Jung et al. (2021) developed a measure called CRISK, which is the expected capital shortfall of a financial institution in a climate stress scenario. The stress testing procedure involves three steps. The first step is to measure the climate risk factor. While there are many ways to measure the climate risk factor, they use stranded asset portfolio return as a proxy for transition risk. The second step is to estimate a time-varying climate beta of financial institutions using the Dynamic Conditional Beta (DCB) model. The third step is to compute CRISK, a function of a given financial firm's size, leverage, and expected equity loss conditional on climate stress. This step is based on the same methodology as SRISK by Acharya et al. (2023), Acharya et al. (2012), and Brownlees and Engle (2017), with the climate factor added as the second factor. Battiston et al. (2017) conduct a network analysis of the exposures of all financial actors to all climate-relevant sectors of the economy and exposures among financial actors across several types of financial instruments. They focus on banks in the eurozone and retrieve data from the ECB Data Warehouse (banks' sectoral exposures carbon leakage risk classification). Later, Nieto (2019) expands the sample by considering more geographical areas (USA, EU, China, Japan, and Switzerland), and he quantifies the (syndicated) loan exposure to elevated environmental risk sectors of the banking system. Both studies converge on similar results. Nieto (2019) indicates the exposure of EU banks at 46.7% of capital by assuming a 3% leverage ratio, while Battiston et al. (2017) indicate an exposure of Euro area banks at 40–54% of capital.

Climate reports provide static exposure but fail to quantify potential losses banks could face under various transition pathways. To assess these risks, forward-looking scenarios are needed (Battiston, 2019; NGFS, 2020). Climate stress testing, an emerging tool in climate finance studies, is one way to achieve this (Battiston et al., 2017; Battiston & Monasterolo, 2019).

5.3 Climate Change: Physical, Transition, and Regulatory Risks

The issue of climate change and its repercussions on global temperatures and the frequency of extreme weather events has assumed an immediate and pressing character. This intricate phenomenon exhibits increasingly discernible connections to human activities as the harmful consequences progressively impinge upon the natural environment, economic operations, and the financial systems of nations across the globe. Rogelj et al. (2018) highlight a substantial gap between the aim of decreasing greenhouse gas (GHG) emissions (Paris Agreement, 2015) and the requirements of climate policies. Based on a brief review of the regulatory path dedicated to the EU banking industry in the last paragraph of the previous chapter, coordination among the regulatory architecture dedicated to climate change risk is still weak. An enforcement mechanism is needed to fill the gap between policies and practices. The European Central Bank (ECB) has been distinguishable in addressing the risks (physical, transition, and regulatory—see Table 5.1) linked to climate change in the banking industry (Eceiza et al., 2020).

Table 5.1 This table shows how climate physical, transition, and regulatory risks are intertwined with credit, market, operational, and other risks in banking (source ECB, 2020)

Banking risks	Climate physical risk – Extreme weather events – Chronic weather patterns	Climate transition risk – Technology and innovation – Market sentiment	Climate regulatory risk – Policies and regulations – Supervision and enforcement
Credit	The probabilities of default (PD) and loss given default (LGD) of exposures within sectors or geographies vulnerable to physical risk may be impacted, for example, by lower collateral valuations in real estate portfolios due to increased flood risk.	Energy efficiency standards may trigger substantial adaptation costs and lower corporate profitability, which can lead to higher PD and lower collateral values.	
Market	Severe physical events may shift market expectations, resulting in sudden repricing, higher volatility, and losses in asset values in some markets.	Transition and regulatory risk drivers may generate an abrupt repricing of securities and derivatives, for example, for products associated with industries affected by asset stranding.	

Table 5.1 (Continued)

Banking risks	Climate physical risk – Extreme weather events – Chronic weather patterns	Climate transition risk – Technology and innovation – Market sentiment	Climate regulatory risk – Policies and regulations – Supervision and enforcement
Operational	Extreme weather events may damage the bank's property, branches, and data centers, disrupting its operations.	Changing consumer sentiment regarding climate issues can lead to reputation and liability risks for the bank due to scandals caused by financing environmentally controversial activities.	
Other risk types (liquidity and business model)	Liquidity risk may be affected if clients withdraw money from their accounts to finance damage repairs.	Transition risk drivers may affect the viability of some business lines and lead to strategic risk for specific business models if the necessary adaptation or diversification is not implemented. For instance, an abrupt repricing of securities due to asset stranding may reduce the value of banks' high-quality liquid assets, thereby affecting liquidity buffers.	

5.3.1 Climate Physical Risk

Physical risks result from the direct impact of climate change on infrastructure, real estate, and business operations (Rivera-Escobar et al., 2022). Extreme weather events like hurricanes, floods, droughts, and wildfires can cause significant harm to banks and result in financial setbacks. Beyond the direct impacts on assets funded by banks, such as real estate or infrastructure projects situated in vulnerable flood-prone or coastal regions, physical risk also indirectly influences borrowers' capacity to service loans due to business disruptions or diminished economic activity.

The banking sector encounters diverse physical risks. Foremost, there is damage to properties and infrastructure. Banks exposed to the real estate sector and mortgages in high-risk areas may experience increased nonperforming loans and decreased asset values following extreme weather events. Banks financing companies heavily reliant on global supply chains may face increased credit risks and loan defaults. Additionally, banks with loan concentrations in vulnerable regions may experience increased credit risks and reduced loan repayment capacity. Addressing these risks requires proactive measures such as investing in resilient infrastructure, implementing effective disaster management strategies, and transitioning to a low-carbon economy. To manage physical risks, banks adopt various strategies. Firstly, risk assessment and scenario analysis are used to assess their exposure to physical risks. This involves analyzing geographic concentrations of assets, vulnerability to climate-related events, and potential impacts on solvency. Scenario analysis helps banks quantify potential losses under different climate scenarios. Secondly, risk mitigation measures are implemented, including adapting lending policies for high-risk sectors or regions, diversifying loan portfolios, and integrating climate resilience criteria into lending decisions. Collateral requirements and insurance coverage may be adjusted to account for climate risks. Lastly, collaboration and the exchange of knowledge play a pivotal role as banks work together with other financial institutions, governments, and research institutions to share best practices and insights regarding the consequences of climate change. These collaborative efforts can result in standardized methodologies for assessing climate-related risks and incorporating climate data into risk models.

5.3.2 *Climate Transition Risk*

Another dimension of climate change risk is transition risk, which arises as a result of the shift to a low-carbon economy. For banks, transition risks have significant implications for their operations and investments. These risks emerge from climate-driven innovations that can disrupt various industries (e.g., the rapid growth of the renewable energy sector). Such risks are often intertwined with policy changes, technology, market dynamics, and consumer preferences. Firstly, transition risks manifest through political and regulatory transformations as governments worldwide enact policies and regulations to mitigate climate change. These measures may encompass carbon pricing mechanisms, renewable energy targets, and emission reduction commitments. As a consequence, specific sectors may undergo diminished profitability or depreciation of assets. Banks heavily exposed to high-carbon sectors or activities may face financial risks if their clients fail to comply with the new regulations. Secondly, there are new dynamics and market changes: transitioning to a low-carbon economy can result in shifts in market demand and investor preferences. Banks with significant exposure to high-carbon sectors may experience reduced profitability and potential loan impairments for financially distressed businesses due to decreased market demand for their products or services. Banks exposed to "stranded assets," such as assets grounded on fossil fuel reserves or coal-fired power plants, which are economically unsustainable, may face significant financial risks, including collateral devaluation and potential loan defaults. They may also be susceptible to reputational harm, legal actions, or disinvestment campaigns initiated by stakeholders advocating for more robust climate-related actions, all because of heightened public consciousness. Thus, they aim to diversify their loan portfolios by augmenting investments in low-carbon sectors, encompassing renewable energy, energy efficiency, and sustainable infrastructure. This strategic shift curtails their vulnerability to high-carbon sectors and aligns their lending practices with low-carbon objectives.

5.3.3 Climate Regulatory Risk

Recent years have witnessed a growing adoption of frameworks such as Task Force on Climate-Related Financial Disclosures (TCFD, 2017) recommendations by banks, which focus on enhancing transparency and facilitating informed decision-making. This involves transparently reporting climate-related risks and opportunities and incorporating climate considerations into their governance and risk management frameworks. Collaboration with industry peers and engagement with regulators and policymakers is essential to ensure a coordinated approach to tackling climate-related financial risks. Regulatory risk arises from government policies and regulations to reduce carbon emissions and address climate change (Fard et al., 2020). Governments worldwide are implementing regulations to curtail greenhouse gas emissions and encourage sustainable practices. These regulatory measures can impact various aspects of banking operations, including risk management strategies, capital requirements, and disclosure obligations. Failure to adhere to these regulations can result in financial penalties, harm to reputation, or legal liabilities. Moreover, banks indirectly encounter regulatory risks linked to climate change through their loan portfolios. This dynamic has the potential to reshape banks' motivations when it comes to credit allocation. Recent research efforts shed light on this topic. For example, Seltzer et al. (2022) have shown that companies with weaker environmental performance, especially in regions with strict environmental regulations, tend to experience wider yield spreads and lower credit ratings. Fard et al. (2020), using a global dataset and focusing on regulatory risk, came to a similar conclusion, indicating that firms subject to stricter environmental regulations face higher lending spreads and reduced credit ratings. Painter (2020), on the other hand, found that US counties more vulnerable to climate risks incur higher underwriting fees and higher initial yields when issuing long-term municipal bonds than counties less exposed to the effects of climate change.

In 2020, the European Central Bank (ECB) published the "Guide on climate-related and environmental risks" to address and mitigate risks while establishing a common framework. This set of rules delineates the principles for a sound and wise supervision of climate and environmental risks within the existing prudential regulation. It provides instructions on how to incorporate these risks into the formulation and implementation of financial institutions' corporate strategies and governance frameworks. It is worth noting that this guide is not legally binding but serves to establish shared principles. Scholarly literature also underscores the evolving operational context for banks. For instance, some researchers propose that banks should integrate climate-related risks into their lending and investment decisions, offer to fund low-carbon projects, and engage with clients to encourage their transition to a decarbonized economy. By doing so, banks can reduce their exposure to corporate regulatory risks.

5.4 Institutional Setting: 2020 EBA Climate Risk Pilot Exercise

The 2020 EBA climate risk pilot exercise conducted in the eurozone is the first tentative, unprecedented central bank exercises aimed at evaluating how well banks are set up to tackle climate-related risks in different scenarios that assessed physical risks (i.e., heatwaves, droughts, and floods, as well as short and long-term risks stemming from the transition to a greener economy). The results show that banks do not yet sufficiently incorporate climate risk into their stress-testing frameworks and internal models despite some progress made since 2020. This stress test is part of our wider climate roadmap and commitment to prepare European banks for the green transition. This exercise is based on a collection of data regarding qualitative and quantitative information to assess the sector's climate risk preparedness and gather best practices for dealing with climate-related risk. During this exercise, they collected data from 29 volunteer-listed EU banks. This information was organized into three modules later during an official stress test conducted by the ECB in 2022, in which 104 banks participated. Here are the three modules:

(i) *Own climate stress-testing capabilities*: they find that around 60% of banks do not yet have a climate risk stress-testing framework (i.e., from the media: the ECB stress test shows that most banks do not include climate risk in credit models (cnbc.com). Most banks do not include climate risk in their credit risk models, and just 20% consider climate risk as a variable when granting loans. Banks currently fall short of best practices, based on which banks should establish climate stress-testing capabilities that include several climate risk transmission channels (e.g., market and credit risks) and portfolios (e.g., corporate and mortgage).
(ii) *Reliance on carbon-emitting sectors*: they find that almost two-thirds of banks' income from nonfinancial corporate customers stems from greenhouse-gas-intensive industries. In many cases, banks' "financed emissions" come from a small number of large counterparties, which increases their exposure to transition risks. Banks often rely on proxies to estimate their exposure to emission-intensive sectors. While this is a good first step to closing the data gaps, banks must increase customer engagement to obtain more accurate data and insights into their clients' transition plans. This is a precondition for banks to gauge and manage their exposure to climate risks in the future.
(iii) *Performance under different scenarios over several time horizons*: the results show that physical risk has a heterogeneous impact across European banks. Findings show that banks' vulnerability to a drought and heat scenario is highly dependent on sectoral activities and the geographical location of their exposures. The impact of this risk materializes through a decrease in sectoral productivity (e.g., in agriculture and construction activities and an increase in loan losses in the affected areas). Similarly, in the flood-risk scenario, real estate

collateral, underlying mortgages, and corporate loans are expected to suffer, particularly in the most affected locations.

I focus on the EBA's first EU-wide pilot exercise on climate risk exposure, where banks voluntarily participated, to eliminate any potential bias from anticipating the impact of the official ECB stress test in 2022. The EBA test results provide evidence about the banking quantification of exposures from a climate perspective (particularly climate transition risk) in corporate financing. To conclude, both EBA and ECB are committed to leading European banks through the green transition. The 2020 EBA climate test findings could be a compass for European banks to boost their climate risk stress-testing capabilities and prepare for the risks and opportunities of transitioning to net zero.

5.5 Research Identification Strategy, Data, and Sample

In this empirical investigation, I consider a sample of volunteer-listed eurozone banks participating in the first EBA pilot exercise dedicated to mapping climate risk. This first identification is based on information collected from several reports disclosed publicly by the EBA in 2021 on its dedicated website (https://www.eba.europa.eu/publications-and-media/press-releases/eba-publishes-results-eu-wide-pilot-exercise-climate-risk). Here, the aims and findings are available, identifying the path for EU banks toward a greener banking system. In one of these reports, I found the 29 volunteer-listed EU banks providing information linked to their climate risk exposure (https://www.eba.europa.eu/sites/default/files/document_library/Publications/Reports/2021/1001589/Mapping%20Climate%20Risk%20-%20Main%20findings%20from%20the%20EU-wide%20pilot%20exercise%20on%20climate%20risk.pdf).

In a further moment, I collected data regarding the amount of loans classified as green lending, taking care to consider the distinction between green loans and sustainability-linked loans. Here, I followed a similar approach to that by Kim et al. (2022), applied at the loan level for a sample of US banks. They used a dataset from Dealscan, assigning two market segment flags corresponding to "Environmental, Social & Governance/Sustainable Linked" and "Green Loan." Refinitiv DealScan uses information from loan agreements, public media releases, and discussions with lenders and borrowers to confirm these loan features. In my case, I looked for the corresponding data provided for eurozone-listed banks in Refinitiv Eikon. I focused on the amount of issued loans per year for each bank, distinguishing loans under two main categories: green loans and sustainability-linked loans. Here, the data provides details about the lender name (bank name), the borrower name (corporate firm), the issued loan amount, the issue and maturity dates of the corresponding loan, the market segment (loan typology), the specific purpose, and the country of domicile. The interesting aspect of this data is that it is possible to know publicly the

Table 5.2 This table reports a sample of listed banks in the eurozone that issue sustainability-linked loans and green loans in the period 2018–2022 based on data retrieved from Refinitiv Eikon. Eleven banks participated voluntarily in the 2020 EBA EU-wide pilot exercise of climate risk exposure

Eurozone listed banks	Country	Isin code	2020 EBA climate test
ERSTE GROUP BANK AG	Austria	AT0000652011	No
DEUTSCHE BANK AG	Germany	DE0005140008	Yes
COMMERZBANK AG	Germany	DE000CBK1001	No
BANCO BILBAO SA	Spain	ES0113211835	Yes
BANCO DE SABADELL SA	Spain	ES0113860A34	No
BANCO SANTANDER SA	Spain	ES0113900J37	Yes
CAIXABANK, S.A.	Spain	ES0140609019	Yes
NORDEA BANK ABP	Finland	FI4000297767	Yes
CREDIT AGRICOLE SA	France	FR0000045072	No
SOCIETE GENERALE	France	FR0000130809	Yes
BNP PARIBAS	France	FR0000131104	Yes
AMUNDI SA	France	FR0004125920	No
MEDIOBANCA S.P.A.	Italy	IT0000062957	No
BPER BANCA S.P.A.	Italy	IT0000066123	No
INTESA SANPAOLO	Italy	IT0000072618	Yes
UNICREDIT SPA	Italy	IT0005239360	Yes
ABN AMRO BANK NV	Netherlands	NL0011540547	Yes
ING GROEP NV	Netherlands	NL0011821202	Yes

several relationships between lenders and borrowers. I dropped those banks that did not issue loans as green or sustainability-linked loans for almost 5 years (2018–2022).

The financial accounting data of the eurozone-listed banks are retrieved from Bankfocus Bureau Van Dijk annually, covering the same period. The EBA exercise on the climate risk exposure of EU banks was initiated in 2020 during the wave of the pandemic crisis. Prior studies observed a connection between the COVID-19 crisis and the decarbonization process, noting that it has boosted banks' active role in supporting the real economy (Dunz et al., 2023).

Based on the data acquired by merging all the datasets, I obtained a final sample composed of 18 listed commercial banks located in the eurozone. I identified 11 banks as volunteer participants in the 2020 EBA EU-wide climate risk exposure pilot exercise (see Table 5.2). These banks are situated in countries like Germany, France, Spain, Italy, the Netherlands, Austria, and Finland. In all these countries, we see that the attention toward climate change and related risks is high, and governments are involved in reducing GHG emissions through corporate policies.

5.6 Methodology

In order to test whether the EBA-wide pilot exercise on climate risk exposure for a group of banks can boost a change in green lending, I decided to employ a difference-in-difference (diff-in-diff) research design to capture the incremental effects of bank transparency, identified in the disclosure of the EBA test results, on the change in green lending (Becchetti et al., 2016; Bonacchi et al., 2022). The empirical model is estimated as follows (Eq. 5.1):

$$\begin{aligned}\Delta \text{Green lending}_{i,c,t} &= \beta 0 + \beta 1 \text{EBAClimate test banks}_{i,c,t} + \beta 2 \,\text{Post}_t \\ &+ \beta 3 \text{EBAClimate test banks}_{i,c,t} \times \text{Post}_t \\ &+ \text{Controls} + \text{Covid19} + \text{Bank} - \text{fixed effects} \\ &+ \text{Country} - \text{fixed effects} + \varepsilon_{i,c,t}\end{aligned} \tag{5.1}$$

where the index i denotes a specific bank, c denotes the country, and t denotes the year. Due to the lag in the publication of financial statements, bank-level data is aligned with the previous year ($t - 1$). The provided model is regression analysis, used to investigate the variation in green lending issued by banks based on several independent variables and control variables (see Table 5.3 for variable definitions). The dependent variable is represented by ΔGreen lending, which is the log change in the loan amount issued by a bank for financing companies based on ESG ratings or for green projects. This bucket of loans mainly comprises sustainability-linked loans (SLL) and green loans (GL). Thus, I ran the test on the log changes in issued sustainability-linked loans (ΔSLL) and the change in green loans (ΔGL).

Table 5.3 Variable definitions

Variable	Definition	Source
Dependent variables		
ΔSLL	The natural logarithm of a bank's annual change in sustainability-linked loans (SLL): it is computed as the log of the amount of sustainability-linked loans from the beginning to the end of year t. SLL data is retrieved from Refinitiv Eikon. I followed Kim et al.'s (2023) approach in identifying this category of loans belonging to the bank's green lending activities. I identified, for several corporate borrowers, the lenders (listed eurozone banks) issuing SLL on a period (2018–2022) around the 2020 EBA EU-wide pilot exercise for bank climate risk exposure. Then I computed the amount per year of SLL issued by each bank.	Refinitiv Eikon Thomson Reuters
ΔGL	The natural logarithm of a bank's annual change in green loans (GL). It is computed as the log of the amount of green loans from the beginning to the end of year t. GL data is retrieved from Refinitiv Eikon. I followed Kim et al.'s (2023) approach in identifying this category of loans belonging to the bank's green lending activities. I identified, for several corporate borrowers, the lenders (listed eurozone banks) issuing GL on a period (2018–2022) around the 2020 EBA EU-wide pilot exercise for bank climate risk exposure. Then I computed the amount per year of GL issued by each bank.	Refinitiv Eikon Thomson Reuters

(continued)

Table 5.3 (continued)

Variable	Definition	Source
Explanatory variables		
EBA Climate test banks	This dummy variable is equal to 1 if listed eurozone banks decided to participate voluntarily in the 2020 EBA EU-wide pilot exercise for bank climate risk exposure and 0 otherwise (https://www.eba.europa.eu/sites/default/files/document_library/Publications/Reports/2021/1001589/Mapping%20Climate%20Risk%20-%20Main%20findings%20from%20the%20EU-wide%20pilot%20exercise%20on%20climate%20risk.pdf).	European Banking Authority (EBA) website
Post	This binary variable indicates the periods following the initiation of the EBA climate test. It takes the value of 1 for 2021–2022 after the identified EBA climate test in 2020 and 0 otherwise.	
Control variables		
Size	The natural logarithm of total assets at the end of the year.	Orbis Bank Focus (Bureau Van Dijk)
Liquidity	Liquid assets to total deposits to total assets.	
Tier1	The total regulatory capital ratio at the end of the year.	
ROA	Return on assets computed as net income to total assets.	
Cost-to-income ratio	Cost-to-income ratio (total non-interest expenses/total non-interest operating income + net interest income + equity-accounted profit/loss – operating).	
Covid19	It is a dummy variable that is equal to 1 if it corresponds to the year 2020 with the highest intensity of the pandemic crisis and 0 otherwise (Bedendo et al., 2023).	

EBA Climate test banks is a dummy variable that is equal to 1 if the bank voluntarily participated in the EBA EU-wide pilot exercise for climate risk exposure initiated in 2020 and concluded in May 2021. This test is still not mandatory, but it is an important tool for measuring how much a bank is exposed to climate physical and transition risks. Moreover, this group of banks could have shown more proactive behaviors toward greenness. The coefficient $\beta 1$ represents how much the treatment affects the variation in the change in green lending.

$Post_t$ is a binary variable that indicates the periods following the initiation of the EBA climate test. It is an indicator variable that takes the value of 1 for 2021–2022 after the identified EBA climate test in 2020 and 0 otherwise. The coefficient $\beta 2$ represents the overall effect of being in the post-EBA period on green lending variations.

$EBA\ Climate\ test\ banks_{i,c,t} \times Post_t$ is the variable of my interest. Within this interaction term, I intend to capture the incremental effects of bank transparency following EBA scrutiny on the issuance of sustainability-linked loans and green loans. The expectation is to find significance once a central bank scrutinizes banks. Still, the direction of this significance could not be univocal since climate risk is an issue for the entire business environment, and the banking industry is no exception. It injects a high level of uncertainty into the valuation process.

I controlled for several factors (*Controls*) that are potentially correlated with the change in green lending, bank transparency (EBA climate test), and country characteristics, as shown in prior banking literature when assessing disclosure effects (Bischof & Daske, 2013). To identify problem banks, bank examiners focused on performance in several areas, including rapid growth, management oversight, risk management, off-balance-sheet exposures, asset quality, loan allowance, and liquidity. To capture these categories, I included the following bank-level variables: *Size* (the natural logarithm of the total assets), because large banks could be more under the supervisor's lens and thus more prone to be more transparent *a priori*. Maintaining adequate levels of liquidity is crucial for banks to withstand unexpected shocks and sudden withdrawals of funds. If a bank has insufficient internal liquidity, it may not be able to maintain a sufficient capital ratio, which can ultimately result in bankruptcy. Banks with lower liquidity ratios often cannot set aside provisions for loan losses to compensate for lower capital levels. Hence, I controlled for *Liquidity* (liquid assets to total deposits) and *Tier1* (the total regulatory capital ratio at the end of the year). I also included *ROA* (return on assets), computed as net income divided by total assets at the end of the year, since poor-quality management should be less profitable and exhibit lower earnings growth on average. The *Cost-to-income ratio* measures a bank's operational efficiency. Decreased efficiency may deplete bank capital, potentially leading to lower "green" lending (Guan et al., 2017). This set of control variables was selected under the criterion that rapid or aggressive growth indicates that a bank may have increased its risk exposure (including climate risk) and, therefore, its susceptibility to a sudden change in economic conditions. Although the sample of eurozone banks is small and could be quite similar since these banks are in the top 50 of European-listed banks (i.e., for size and business model), I decided to account for time trend factor clustering standard errors at the bank and year levels to control for potential bias in the estimates and via the inclusion of several types of fixed effects. The period under examination is 2020, which represents one of the most disruptive moments in economic history because of the wave of COVID-19 leading to the pandemic crisis. Therefore, I included Covid19 as a dummy variable equal to 1 if it corresponds to 2020 indicating the highest moment of intensity of the Pandemic crisis, and 0 otherwise (Bedendo et al., 2023). Furthermore, I included *bank- and country-fixed effects*, which help control for further differences in diversification strategies and country-specific time-independent factors (Amir et al., 2016). Thus, to alleviate the possibility that the EBA climate test could also be affected by the explosion of the pandemic crisis in 2020 and additional ECB initiatives, I employed country-fixed effects for all banks headquartered in a specific country.

5.7 Empirical Results

This section presents my main empirical findings: descriptive statistics and diff-in-diff results. Table 5.4 (Panel A—full sample, Panel B—treatment sample, and Panel C—control sample) reports the summary statistics (mean, standard deviation, P25, median, and P75) of the dependent variables and control variables for a sample of

Table 5.4 Summary descriptive statistics. Panel A (full sample), Panel B (treatment sample), and Panel C (control sample) of this table report the descriptive statistics (mean, standard deviation, percentile 25th, median, percentile 75th) for the variables (dependent variable and control variables) employed in the main analyses. See Table 5.3 for the variable definitions

	N	Mean	SD	p25	Median	p75
Panel A. Full sample comprises 18 listed eurozone banks covering 2018–2022.						
ΔSLL	90	0.243	0.738	0.000	0.221	0.271
ΔGL	90	0.099	0.564	0.000	0.076	0.101
Size	90	26.94	1.179	26.34	27.21	27.91
Liquidity	90	0.345	0.145	0.270	0.331	0.368
Tier1	90	15.83	3.318	13.83	15.00	16.21
ROA	90	0.006	0.008	0.002	0.004	0.006
Cost-to-income ratio	90	0.664	0.115	0.581	0.637	0.719
Panel B. Treatment sample comprises 11 listed eurozone banks covering 2018–2022. These banks do green lending and voluntarily participated in the 2020 EBA EU-wide pilot exercise for bank climate risk exposure.						
ΔSLL	55	0.242	0.707	0.000	0.219	0.250
ΔGL	55	0.126	0.684	0.000	0.110	0.129
Size	55	27.45	0.616	27.03	27.51	27.93
Liquidity	55	0.333	0.105	0.275	0.332	0.401
Tier1	55	16.39	3.862	13.89	15.31	17.31
ROA	55	0.004	0.002	0.002	0.004	0.005
Cost-to-income ratio	55	0.660	0.120	0.566	0.624	0.718
Panel C. The control sample is composed of 7 listed eurozone banks covering the period 2018–2022. These banks do green lending but did not participate in the 2020 EBA EU-wide pilot exercise for bank climate risk exposure.						
ΔSLL	35	0.245	0.795	0.000	0.231	0.275
ΔGL	35	0.056	0.297	0.000	0.032	0.061
Size	35	26.11	1.390	25.09	26.18	26.95
Liquidity	35	0.364	0.194	0.241	0.317	0.368
Tier1	35	14.92	1.894	13.83	14.27	15.90
ROA	35	0.009	0.013	0.002	0.004	0.009
Cost-to-income ratio	35	0.672	0.107	0.600	0.665	0.735

18 Euro-listed banks covering the period 2018–2022. The explanatory variable is *EBA Climate test banks*, taking the value of 1 if the banks of my sample voluntarily participated in the 2020 EBA EU-wide pilot exercise for bank climate risk exposure and 0 otherwise. The descriptive statistics show that the two groups of banks (treatment and control) are quite similar. Both groups are involved in issuing sustainability-linked loans and green loans.

The change in sustainability-linked loans is (quite) the same between the treatment and control samples ($\Delta SLL = 0.242$ for the treated banks, $\Delta SLL = 0.245$ for the control banks), while the change in green loans is higher for the banks included in the treatment sample compared to those in the control sample ($\Delta GL = 0.126$ for the treated banks, $\Delta GL = 0.056$ for the control banks). Table 5.5 reports the

Table 5.5 Differences in mean. This table reports statistical differences in the mean of the variables between the two samples (treatment vs. control)

	Treatment: mean	Control: mean	Difference in mean: treatment-control *t*-stat
ΔSLL	0.242	0.245	−0.002 [−0.01]
ΔGL	0.126	0.056	0.069 [0.56]
Size	27.45	26.11	0.134*** [6.26]
Liquidity	0.333	0.364	−0.031 [−0.97]
Tier1	16.39	14.92	1.462** [2.05]
ROA	0.004	0.009	−0.005*** [−3.18]
Cost-to-income ratio	0.660	0.672	−0.012 [−0.48]

*, **, and *** denote significance at the 10%, 5%, and 1% level, respectively

Table 5.6 Matrix correlation

	ΔSLL	ΔGL	Size	Liquidity	Tier1	ROA	Cost-to-income ratio
ΔSLL	1						
ΔGL	0.164	1					
Size	0.096	0.090	1				
Liquidity	0.014	0.123	0.362***	1			
Tier1	−0.062	−0.085	0.013	−0.092	1		
ROA	−0.194	−0.045	−0.680***	−0.029	−0.158	1	
Cost-to-income ratio	0.084	0.158	0.039	−0.068	−0.099	−0.220*	1

*, **, and *** denote significance at the 10%, 5%, and 1% level, respectively

differences in mean for the variables employed in empirical tests between the treatment and the control samples. We see that except for *Size*, *Tier1*, and *ROA*, there are no differences in mean for other variables between the treatment and control samples. Table 5.6 presents the results of the correlation matrix. The results show that the dependent variables (*ΔSLL* and *ΔGL*) are not correlated with the control variables (*Size*, *Liquidity*, *Tier1*, *ROA*, and *Cost-to-income ratio*).

Panel A of Table 5.7 presents the first results obtained from the diff-in-diff regression model (Eq. 5.1) by employing, as dependent variables, the log change in sustainability-linked loans (*ΔSLL*) and the log change in green loans (*ΔGL*) with no fixed effects. The interaction of my interest (*EBA Climate test banks* × *Post*) is positively and significantly associated with *ΔSLL* (0.730***) and *ΔGL* (0.470*). From this first set of results, I interpret that listed eurozone banks voluntarily participating in the EBA stress tests show a propensity to do more green lending after the scrutiny. Table 5.7 Panel B presents further results from the diff-in-diff regressions, including the bank- and country-level fixed effects. We see that the results hold, and again, the magnitude is stronger on the log change in sustainability-linked loans (0.726***) compared to the log change in green loans (0.458*). Table 5.7 Panel C presents the results obtained from the diff-in-diff regression model (Eq. 5.1) by

Table 5.7 Diff-in-diff results

	(1)	(2)
	ΔSLL	ΔGL
Panel A. This table presents the results obtained from employing Eq. 5.1 without fixed effects. T-statistics, based on two-way cluster-robust standard errors at the bank and year levels, are presented below the coefficient estimates.		
EBA Climate test banks	−0.282*	−0.014
	[−1.93]	[−0.14]
EBA Climate test banks × Post	0.730***	0.470*
	[3.18]	[1.99]
Post	−0.090	−0.133
	[−0.60]	[−1.16]
Size	−0.078	−0.043
	[−1.09]	[−0.51]
Liquidity	0.119	0.614
	[0.12]	[1.03]
Tier1	−0.031	−0.019
	[−1.52]	[−1.51]
ROA	−0.229*	−0.137
	[−1.98]	[−0.14]
Cost-to-income ratio	0.066	0.836
	[0.09]	[0.88]
_cons	1.870	0.190
	[1.38]	[0.14]
Bank FE	No	No
Country FE	No	No
Cluster SE	Bank & Year	Bank & Year
Adj. R^2	0.092	0.045
N	90	90

	(1)	(2)
	ΔSLL	ΔGL
Panel B. This table presents the results obtained from employing Eq. 5.1, including bank- and country-fixed effects. T-statistics, based on two-way cluster-robust standard errors at the bank and year levels, are presented below the coefficient estimates.		
EBA Climate test banks × Post	0.726***	0.458**
	[3.32]	[2.12]
Post	−0.108	−0.189
	[−0.59]	[−1.16]
Size	−0.139	0.055
	[−0.78]	[0.41]
Liquidity	0.751	0.587
	[0.71]	[1.01]

(continued)

Table 5.7 (continued)

	(1)	(2)
	ΔSLL	ΔGL
Tier1	−0.033	−0.032
	[−1.22]	[−1.65]
ROA	−0.332	−0.111
	[−1.53]	[−0.63]
Cost-to-income ratio	0.219	2.353
	[0.23]	[1.54]
_cons	2.278	−1.972
	[0.86]	[−0.73]
Bank FE	Yes	Yes
Country FE	Yes	Yes
Cluster SE	Bank & Year	Bank & Year
Adj. R^2	0.021	0.071
N	90	90

	(1)	(2)
	ΔSLL	ΔGL
Panel C. This table presents the results obtained from employing Eq. 5.1, including (1) the dummy variable *Covid19* to control for any confounding time trends because of the Pandemic crisis and (2) bank- and country-fixed effects. T-statistics, based on two-way cluster-robust standard errors at the bank and year levels, are presented below the coefficient estimates.		
EBA Climate test banks × Post	0.531**	0.223
	[2.07]	[1.30]
Post	−0.055	0.151
	[−0.22]	[0.84]
Size	−0.108	0.049
	[−0.64]	[0.39]
Liquidity	0.513	0.504
	[0.51]	[0.88]
Tier1	−0.038	−0.039**
	[−1.43]	[−2.03]
ROA	−0.297	−0.094
	[−1.55]	[−0.57]
Cost-to-income ratio	0.544	2.137
	[0.59]	[1.45]
Covid19	−0.463**	−0.250
	[−2.38]	[−1.65]
_cons	1.891	−1.618
	[0.75]	[−0.62]
Bank FE	Yes	Yes
Country FE	Yes	Yes

(continued)

Table 5.7 (continued)

	(1)	(2)
	ΔSLL	ΔGL
Cluster SE	Bank & Year	Bank & Year
Adj. R^2	0.076	0.088
N	90	90

*, **, and *** denote significance at the 10%, 5%, and 1% level, respectively

including not only the fixed effects at the bank and country levels but also the dummy variable Covid19 to control for any confounding time trends determined by the pandemic crisis in the year 2020. In this last case, we can observe a positive and significant effect only on the log change in sustainability-linked loans (0.531**), while there is no longer any significant effect on the log change in green loans. These last findings indicate that EBA transparency has led banks to have more trust in using borrowers' environmental information when issuing loans, such as sustainability-linked loans, which do not necessarily aim to finance something "green" (i.e., green loans).

Figure 5.1 (Panels A and B) presents a parallel trend analysis (Armstrong et al., 2022) between the listed eurozone banks participating in the 2020 EBA climate stress test (treatment sample) and the listed eurozone banks not participating (control sample). Specifically, I separately estimate yearly regressions for the years 2018 through 2022, respectively, with the year 2020 being the "shock" event. The regression uses *EBA Climate test banks*, the control variables (including *Covid19*), and bank- and country-fixed effects from the equation. The figures show the plot of the coefficients on *EBA Climate test banks* for the regressions on *Log change in sustainability linked loans* (Panel A) and *Log change in green loans* (Panel B). Panel A (*Log change in sustainability linked loans*) shows that there are no discernible patterns nor significant coefficients on the coefficients for *EBA Climate test banks* for the preperiod (2018–2019), thus validating the parallel trend assumption. Panel B (*Log change in green loans*) shows that there are no discernible patterns nor significant coefficients for *EBA Climate test banks* for the preperiod (2018–2019) and no incremental significant effects in the postperiod (2021–2022). The parallel trend analysis confirms the results reported in Table 5.7 Panel C, showing an incremental effect only when I regress on the log change in sustainability-linked loans (ΔSLL).

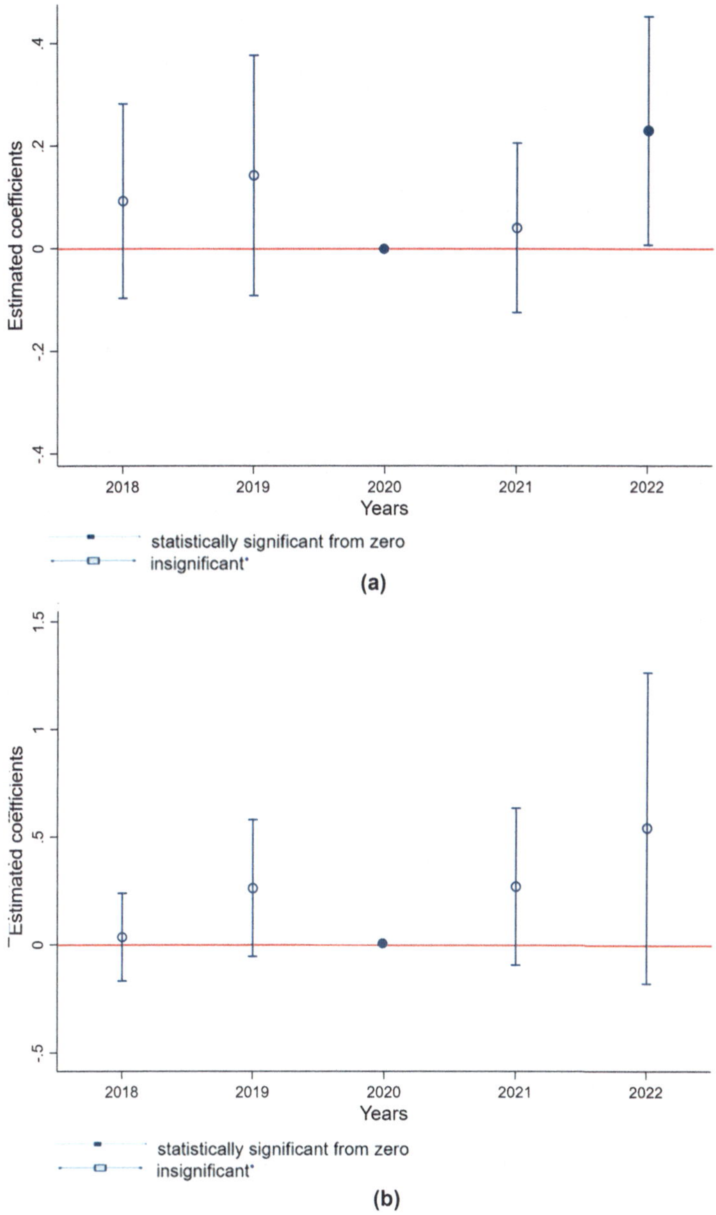

Fig. 5.1 Parallel trend analysis between treatment and control samples. This figure plots yearly treatment point estimates based on Eq. 5.1 for the log change in sustainability-linked loans (ΔSLL—Panel A) and the log change in green loans (ΔGL—Panel B). 2020 is the year when EBA begins the first EU-wide exercise to map banks' climate risk exposure. The years 2018–2019 correspond to the preshock period, while the years 2021–2022 represent the postshock period. The treatment sample is composed of the 11 listed eurozone banks that voluntarily participated in the EBA climate stress test, while the control sample is composed of seven listed eurozone banks not scrutinized by the EBA. *Panel A.* Log change in sustainability-linked loans. *Panel B.* Log change in green loans

5.8 Discussion and Conclusion

In this analysis, I first examine the effects of scrutiny regarding bank climate risk exposure on the green lending change of a sample of listed eurozone banks. In doing this, I leverage the 2020 EBA EU-wide pilot exercise to map the banks' climate risk. Following the identification strategy proposed by Kim et al. (2023), I consider those banks that, from 2018, were issuing sustainability-linked and green loans. By controlling for several factors at the bank level (size, liquidity, Tier1, ROA, and cost-to-income ratio) and time-cofounding events like the COVID-19 disruptive wave, and including bank- and country-fixed effects, I find that banks, following EBA scrutiny, are more prone to issue sustainability-linked loans instead of green loans. These findings suggest that banks showing a higher level of transparency by disclosing their climate risk exposure through the EBA climate stress test are more likely to consider borrowers' environmental disclosure to issue sustainability-linked loans where the lending process does not meet the aim of financing a green project. Unlike green loans, where the process is entirely based on recognizing a loan for financing something "green," sustainability-linked loans do not necessarily lead borrowers toward a constrained decarbonization process. These results assume a significant connotation if we consider the call to make banks responsible for decarbonizing the whole economy. Thus, banks still struggle to guide companies toward a totally green economic approach. However, the monitoring effect of EBA encourages banks to engage in general green lending, meeting the regulator's expectations (see the EU Capital Requirements Directive (CRD) IV for new measures to increase banking transparency, Longo et al., 2024).

This research investigation can contribute in a twofold way. First, this study adds to the large literature dedicated to bank transparency and the role of stress test disclosures (Bischof & Daske, 2013; Petrella & Resti, 2013). Therefore, I consider the first climate stress test exercised by the European Banking Authority and following by the European Central Bank on a group of European listed banks. Thus, we see how central banks, as a safe guardian of the whole economy, contribute day by day to increasing the bank transparency level. Second, it contributes to providing empirical evidence on green lending, where banks are called to play an active role in reducing carbon emissions (Giannetti et al., 2023; Kim et al., 2022). Nowadays, EU banks continue to finance brown industries, but the regulation dedicated to climate change risks is pushing the same banks to welcome more and more "green" borrowers.

Besides contributing to the academic literature, these findings can also be informative for managers of central banks and other stakeholders involved in the transition toward decarbonization. As with any study, even this empirical research is not free from limitations. Indeed, the sample of listed eurozone banks is still small because of issues on data availability, and no balancing techniques between the treatment and control samples have been employed to avoid manipulating the data and, consequently, the results of the empirical tests (Ernstberger et al., 2017).

References

Acharya, V. V., Jager, M., & Steffen, S. (2023). *Contingent Credit Under Stress* (No. w31909). National Bureau of Economic Research.

Acharya, V. V., Pedersen, L. H., Philippon, T., & Richardson, M. (2012). How to calculate systemic risk surcharges. In *Quantifying systemic risk* (pp. 175–212). University of Chicago Press.

Amir, E., Carabias, J. M., Jona, J., & Livne, G. (2016). Fixed-effects in empirical accounting research. *Available at SSRN 2634089.*

Armstrong, C., Kepler, J. D., Samuels, D., & Taylor, D. (2022). Causality redux: The evolution of empirical methods in accounting research and the growth of quasi-experiments. *Journal of Accounting and Economics*, 101521.

Battiston, S. (2019). The importance of being forward-looking: Managing financial stability in the face of climate risk. *Financial Stability Review, 23*, 39–48.

Battiston, S., Mandel, A., Monasterolo, I., Schütze, F., & Visentin, G. (2017). A climate stress-test of the financial system. *Nature Climate Change, 7*(4), 283–288.

Battiston, S., & Monasterolo, I. (2019). A climate risk assessment of sovereign bonds' portfolio. *SSRN Electronic Journal, July, 1*, 1–33.

Becchetti, L., Ciciretti, R., & Paolantonio, A. (2016). The cooperative bank difference before and after the global financial crisis. *Journal of International Money and Finance, 69*, 224–246.

Bedendo, M., Garcia-Appendini, E., & Siming, L. (2023). Managers' cultural origin and corporate response to an economic shock. *Journal of Corporate Finance, 80*, 102412.

Bischof, J., & Daske, H. (2013). Mandatory disclosure, voluntary disclosure, and stock market liquidity: Evidence from the EU bank stress tests. *Journal of Accounting Research, 51*(5), 997–1029.

Bonacchi, M., Klein, A., Longo, S., & Strampelli, G. (2022). The effects of credible voluntary disclosures: Institutional investor engagement and investees' ESG performances. *European Corporate Governance Institute-Law Working Paper*, (622).

Brownlees, C., & Engle, R. F. (2017). SRISK: A conditional capital shortfall measure of systemic risk. *The Review of Financial Studies, 30*(1), 48–79.

Dunz, N., Essenfelder, A. H., Mazzocchetti, A., Monasterolo, I., & Raberto, M. (2023). Compounding COVID-19 and climate risks: The interplay of banks' lending and government's policy in the shock recovery. *Journal of Banking & Finance, 152*, 106306.

Eceiza, J., Harreis, H., Härtl, D., & Viscardi, S. (2020). *Banking imperatives for managing climate risk*. McKinsey & Company.

Ellahie, A. (2013). Capital market consequences of EU bank stress tests. *Available at SSRN 2157715.*

Ernstberger, J., Link, B., Stich, M., & Vogler, O. (2017). The real effects of mandatory quarterly reporting. *The Accounting Review, 92*(5), 33–60.

Fard, A., Javadi, S., & Kim, I. (2020). Environmental regulation and the cost of bank loans: International evidence. *Journal of Financial Stability, 51*, 100797.

Fernandes, M., Igan, D., & Pinheiro, M. (2020). March madness in Wall Street: (What) does the market learn from stress tests? *Journal of Banking & Finance, 112*, 105250.

Giannetti, M., Jasova, M., Loumioti, M., & Mendicino, C. (2023). "Glossy Green" Banks: The Disconnect Between Environmental Disclosures and Lending Activities.

Guan, R., Zheng, H., Hu, J., Fang, Q., & Ren, R. (2017). The higher carbon intensity of loans, the higher non-performing loan ratio: The case of China. *Sustainability, 9*(4), 667.

Huang, B., Punzi, M. T., & Wu, Y. (2021). Do banks price environmental transition risks? Evidence from a quasi-natural experiment in China. *Journal of Corporate Finance, 69*, 101983.

Jung, H., Engle, R. F., & Berner, R. B. (2021). *Climate stress testing* (No. 977). Staff Report.

Kim, S., Kumar, N., Lee, J., & Oh, J. (2022). ESG lending. In *Proceedings of Paris December 2021 Finance Meeting EUROFIDAI-ESSEC, European Corporate Governance Institute–Finance Working Paper* (No. 817).

Longo, S., Fabrizi, M., & Parbonetti, A. (2024). Market reaction to EU CRD IV regulation in the banking industry. *Research in International Business and Finance*.

Nieto, M. J. (2019). Banks, climate risk and financial stability. *Journal of Financial Regulation and Compliance, 27*(2), 243–262.

Painter, M. (2020). An inconvenient cost: The effects of climate change on municipal bonds. *Journal of Financial Economics, 135*(2), 468–482.

Petrella, G., & Resti, A. (2013). Supervisors as information producers: Do stress tests reduce bank opaqueness? *Journal of Banking & Finance, 37*(12), 5406–5420.

Reinders, H. J., Schoenmaker, D., & van Dijk, M. (2023). A finance approach to climate stress testing. *Journal of International Money and Finance, 131*, 102797.

Rivera-Escobar, O., Escobar, J. W., & Manotas, D. F. (2022). Measurement of systemic risk in the Colombian banking sector. *Risks, 10*(1), 22.

Rogelj, J., Popp, A., Calvin, K. V., Luderer, G., Emmerling, J., Gernaat, D., et al. (2018). Scenarios towards limiting global mean temperature increase below 1.5 C. *Nature Climate Change, 8*(4), 325–332.

Seltzer, L. H., Starks, L., & Zhu, Q. (2022). *Climate regulatory risk and corporate bonds* (No. w29994). National Bureau of Economic Research.

Chapter 6
Final Remarks

6.1 Summary

This monograph offers a comprehensive understanding of how banking disclosure has evolved in the last decades, shaping banks' behaviors and, mainly, investors' decision-making. The banking industry is the most regulated sector and, consequently, the most scrutinized. This is because of its fundamental economic role in supporting economic development growth through lending activities while simultaneously holding households' savings. Banks attract the attention of many stakeholders, not just investors, who desire a healthy and sound banking system. Despite various external mechanisms and pressure from stakeholders to monitor banks, a series of negative events have still overwhelmed the banking system. Notably, the 2008 financial crisis, which resulted in significant losses for banks, has cast a long shadow over recent decades. Furthermore, a series of scandals and frauds, driven by poor governance and reiterated earnings management practices, has eroded general confidence in the banking system. These were the main factors that led to the implementation of stringent regulations to ensure financial stability. For banks to be more stable, the regulator began to promote transparency through two activities—more timely and accurate reporting, on the one hand, and greater disclosure of information, on the other—to obtain a more accurate picture of banks' financial performance. Supervision was enhanced with new tools requiring banks to provide detailed reports on risk exposure and asset quality, particularly regarding loan portfolios (Bischof et al., 2021; Granja & Leuz, 2024). As opacity was seen as a major factor in the severity of the 2008 financial crisis, disclosure became crucial for increasing bank transparency.

In the first two chapters of this monograph, I outline the progression from voluntary to mandatory disclosure, highlighting how banks alternate between the two based on strategic decisions made by their management. In these chapters, the goal was not to figure out which solution was best for banks that were at the crossroads

© The Author(s), under exclusive license to Springer Nature Switzerland AG 2025

S. Longo, *Disclosure in Banking*, SIDREA Series in Accounting and Business Administration, https://doi.org/10.1007/978-3-031-84196-5_6

of choosing between voluntary and mandatory disclosures. Certainly, the consensus is that with mandatory disclosure, banks no longer choose to hide bad information. However, any disclosure—voluntary or mandatory, investor-friendly or not—makes banks more transparent (Nier, 2005).

Much of banking disclosure focuses on conveying the bank's risks through various accounting reporting practices. The third chapter examines how disclosure interacts with both accounting and banking regulations (Bertomeu et al., 2023), emphasizing the need for the disclosures to align with regulatory requirements without distorting or obscuring the true financial situation. Unfortunately, this is exactly what happened with the collapse of some banks (i.e., Silicon Valley Bank, Credit Suisse) in March 2023, where the debate on the truthfulness of disclosure concerning reporting activities resurfaced. These critical issues have highlighted the fragile link between the two different regulations. On the one hand, with accounting, we aim to inform the markets timely and accurately; on the other hand, with banking regulation, we want to safeguard stability. Accounting conservatism and banking prudentialism can generate distorting effects, where too much disclosure does not necessarily mean good quality of information nor guarantee the prevention of banking failures. To all this, we need to add the disclosure required by supervisors, such as national and supranational central banks, which test banks' ability to absorb any financial turbulence through their resilience, considering regulatory capital, liquidity, and funding robustness (Bischof & Daske, 2013; Petrella & Resti, 2013). The results of stress tests and transparency exercises are based on banks' disclosure reports, rather than asset quality assessments, and play a crucial role in shaping market reactions based on investor perceptions. Therefore, too much disclosure could lead to the danger of bank runs, rather than sudden vulnerabilities in the financial markets, triggered by panic and irrationality.

Risk disclosure is an important activity through which banks communicate both financial and nonfinancial aspects. I initially emphasized what, how, and when banks have to disclose risk financial information, identifying the complexity that banks have to face to comply with all these rules. At the end of Chap. 3, I describe the shift from voluntary to mandatory nonfinancial information, where, because of EU Directive 2014, European banks were forced to produce regularly standardized environmental, social, and governance (ESG) reports. ESG comprises environmental, social, and governance items that include a set of other risks that banks should consider and manage. While governance has always been an important banking aspect, environmental and social (E&S) disclosures have been much more emphasized in light of pollution and racial-gender discrimination scandals. This has represented a notable change in terms of communication for both financial and nonfinancial information, requiring new expertise and skills (Löw et al., 2019; Korca et al., 2021; Veltri et al., 2023). This occurred around the same time, with the adoption of the Capital Requirements Directive (CRD) IV in 2013 and the Mandatory Non-Financial Disclosure Reporting Directive in 2014. Consequently, empirical research finds it challenging to disentangle the distinct effects of each regulation (Downar et al., 2021; Fiechter et al., 2022).

Chap. 4 focuses on the evolution of environmental disclosure in the context of growing climate change risk awareness. For banks, understanding environmental issues is crucial, as their borrowers generate information centered around the sustainability of their businesses. At the same time, banks are expected to promote green projects. This highlights the dual role of banks: they aim to generate more sustainable (green) profits while penalizing borrowers who are not sufficiently sustainable (Giannetti et al., 2023). Additionally, banks have the role of promoting their green initiatives and influencing social aspects within local communities (Houston & Shan, 2022). Thus, banks are not only key players in shaping the banking market but also in influencing broader socio-economic changes, with the potential for more political involvement. Unlike the slower process of educating the public on environmental and social issues, banks can influence corporate behaviour quickly. Recent studies show how banks are adapting their lending practices, becoming more transparent about environmental, social, and governance (ESG) factors, even if this means lower profits in the short term (Basu et al., 2022). Moreover, banks with a strong ESG focus attract borrowers who share similar sustainability values (Hauptmann, 2017).

These new mechanisms have created evolving banking scenarios in which banks have little choice but to adapt. Not only are they engaging in less earnings management due to stricter accounting and banking regulations, but they must also factor in the growing risk of natural disasters. If banks continue to finance borrowers who fail to adopt sustainable practices and environmentally friendly corporate policies, they risk deteriorating the quality of their loan portfolios. In today's climate, sustainability is not just a matter of ethical responsibility but also of managing the financial impact of climate-related risks. Banks must now integrate these risks into their corporate risk management strategies to better prepare for the damages caused by natural disasters, which further highlight the urgent need to address climate risk.

In Chap. 5, I examine whether a group of European listed banks are incentivized to increase green lending when subjected to a specific climate risk stress test. The 2020 European Banking Authority (EBA) evaluation required banks to disclose how they assess climate risk and address environmental factors within their operations, particularly in lending activities. According to the EBA's findings, EU banks still struggle to effectively manage climate risk and promote green initiatives among their borrowers. However, banks that underwent the 2020 climate risk stress test were encouraged to adopt more robust methodologies for managing climate risks and providing environmental disclosures. This shift led to a notable increase in green lending following the release of the test results. The transparency fostered by a disclosure enforcement mechanism, such as the EBA's climate stress test (Granja & Leuz, 2024), seems to reward banks committed to improving their management of complex climate risks in anticipation of future green lending. This serves as a warning for banks that have not been scrutinized, as they too must manage climate risks effectively using both financial and non-financial data on borrowers. Given the increasing interdependence of these two types of information, they can no longer be treated as separate entities.

6.2 Potential Avenues for Future Research

The recent economic instability triggered by the COVID-19 crisis (2020–2022) and the subsequent collapse of, specifically, two banks (i.e., Silicon Valley Bank and Credit Suisse) in March 2023 has raised many doubts among regulators, policymakers, and academics about the role played by disclosure, especially when it is mandatory. We have learned from prior studies that this is not the complete solution to any banking problems linked to financial stability. Surely, there has been a combination of events that allows us to consider more deeply the role of disclosure in banking and to understand how it can shape banks' behaviors. For instance, Berger and Demirgüç-Kunt (2021) invite researchers to explore the measures addressed to the banking industry during the COVID-19 crisis. Thus, the Pandemic crisis has been regarded as one of the most significant exogenous shocks for examining the economic impacts and corporate behaviours triggered by this health emergency. Banks play a crucial role in the global economy, and their actions during this period are of particular interest. It is essential for banks to disclose the specific programs they implemented in response to the Pandemic, as this transparency can help assess whether any changes in their monitoring practices or reporting activities may have compromised financial stability.

The COVID-19 emergency has injected a particular boost around ESG topics (Dunz et al., 2021), leading banks to be much more engaged in the decarbonization process (Gurol & Lagasio, 2022; Wang, 2023). Recent papers have shown the difficulties banks face in issuing only green loans, thereby abandoning brown borrowers. It is necessary to explore further the mechanisms that could lead banks to support a more sustainable economic development while maintaining good levels of profitability (Basu et al., 2022; Giannetti et al., 2023). Environmental and social issues are central to banking actions, with banks being called upon to shape corporate behaviors. Banks are also engaged in understanding how to capture borrowers' greenwashing. There is an emerging line of research that examines how to identify and measure the phenomenon of greenwashing in banking (Liu & Li, 2024). This is extremely important if we think about how much it can affect the quality of bank loan portfolios. Furthermore, banks' new role in the transition to decarbonization may imply the use of new technologies and, consequently, a change in business models. Understanding the business model is fundamental, and its opacity may cause further financial crises (Hryckiewicz & Kozłowski, 2017). The integration of artificial intelligence is set to revolutionize both financial and non-financial disclosure practices (Musleh Al-Sartawi et al., 2022; Shiyyab et al., 2023), as well as transform the banking labour market. Algorithms are increasingly being used not only for data analysis but also in the recruitment and management of human resources, fundamentally altering how banks operate and make decisions about their workforce.

As a concluding remark, we agree that researchers are called to make new efforts to unveil hidden information behind mandatory disclosure, especially about climate change and workforce diversity, which could lead to a more dangerous financial crisis. Furthermore, we see that a crisis situation can totally dismantle some human and regulatory beliefs because the economic scenario is contaminated by many factors that are beyond human control. Through research, we can learn from the past and look to the future with more confidence, focusing on banking disclosure through which business is known in the world.

References

Basu, S., Vitanza, J., Wang, W., & Zhu, X. R. (2022). Walking the walk? Bank ESG disclosures and home mortgage lending. *Review of Accounting Studies, 27*(3), 779–821.

Berger, A. N., & Demirgüç-Kunt, A. (2021). Banking research in the time of COVID-19. *Journal of Financial Stability, 57*, 100939.

Bertomeu, J., Mahieux, L., & Sapra, H. (2023). Interplay between accounting and prudential regulation. *The Accounting Review, 98*(1), 29–53.

Bischof, J., & Daske, H. (2013). Mandatory disclosure, voluntary disclosure, and stock market liquidity: Evidence from the EU bank stress tests. *Journal of Accounting Research, 51*(5), 997–1029.

Bischof, J., Laux, C., & Leuz, C. (2021). Accounting for financial stability: Bank disclosure and loss recognition in the financial crisis. *Journal of Financial Economics, 141*(3), 1188–1217.

Downar, B., Ernstberger, J., Reichelstein, S., Schwenen, S., & Zaklan, A. (2021). The impact of carbon disclosure mandates on emissions and financial operating performance. *Review of Accounting Studies, 26*(3), 1137–1175.

Dunz, N., Emambakhsh, T., Hennig, T., Kaijser, M., Kouratzoglou, C., & Salleo, C. (2021). ECB's Economy-Wide Climate Stress Test. *ECB Occasional Paper*, (2021/281).

Fiechter, P., Hitz, J. M., & Lehmann, N. (2022). Real effects of a widespread CSR reporting mandate: Evidence from the European Union's CSR Directive. *Journal of Accounting Research, 60*(4), 1499–1549.

Giannetti, M., Jasova, M., Loumioti, M., & Mendicino, C. (2023). "Glossy green" banks: The disconnect between environmental disclosures and lending activities. *ECB Working Paper*, (2023/2882).

Granja, J., & Leuz, C. (2024). The death of a regulator: Strict supervision, bank lending, and business activity. *Journal of Financial Economics, 158*, 103871.

Gurol, B., & Lagasio, V. (2022). Women board members' impact on ESG disclosure with environment and social dimensions: Evidence from the European banking sector. *Social Responsibility Journal, 19*(1), 211–228.

Hauptmann, C. (2017). Corporate sustainability performance and bank loan pricing: It pays to be good, but only when banks are too. *Saïd Business School WP, 20*.

Houston, J. F., & Shan, H. (2022). Corporate ESG profiles and banking relationships. *The Review of Financial Studies, 35*(7), 3373–3417.

Hryckiewicz, A., & Kozłowski, Ł. (2017). Banking business models and the nature of financial crisis. *Journal of International Money and Finance, 71*, 1–24.

Korca, B., Costa, E., & Farneti, F. (2021). From voluntary to mandatory non-financial disclosure following Directive 2014/95/EU: An Italian case study. *Accounting in Europe, 18*(3), 353–377.

Liu, Z., & Li, X. (2024). The impact of bank fintech on ESG greenwashing. *Finance Research Letters, 62*, 105199.

Löw, E., Klein, D., & Pavicevac, A. (2019). Corporate Social Responsibility Reports of European Banks–An Empirical Analysis of the Disclosure Quality and its Determinants.

Musleh Al-Sartawi, A. M., Hussainey, K., & Razzaque, A. (2022). The role of artificial intelligence in sustainable finance. *Journal of Sustainable Finance & Investment*, 1–6.

Nier, E. W. (2005). Bank stability and transparency. *Journal of Financial Stability, 1*(3), 342–354.

Petrella, G., & Resti, A. (2013). Supervisors as information producers: Do stress tests reduce bank opaqueness? *Journal of Banking & Finance, 37*(12), 5406–5420.
Shiyyab, F. S., Alzoubi, A. B., Obidat, Q. M., & Alshurafat, H. (2023). The impact of artificial intelligence disclosure on financial performance. *International Journal of Financial Studies, 11*(3), 115.
Veltri, S., Cristiano, E., & Ferraro, O. (2023). Examining the quality of the consolidated mandatory non-financial statements of a cooperative banking group: A longitudinal analysis. *Corporate Social Responsibility and Environmental Management, 30*(4), 1573–1587.
Wang, L. L. (2023). Transmission effects of ESG disclosure regulations through bank lending networks. *Journal of Accounting Research, 61*(3), 935–978.